A Planners Guide to Community and Regional Food Planning

Samina Raja, Branden Born, and Jessica Kozlowski Russell

TABLE OF CONTENTS

CHAPTER 1

Food, Healthy Eating, and Planning

ood nourishes us, enriches our celebrations, and sustains life itself. Yet not everyone in the U.S. has access to foods that nourish. Some of us live in neighborhoods where grocery stores carry a greater variety of potato chips than vegetables, while some of us cannot afford vegetables, even when they are available. The quality of food environments in places where people live, work, and play carries significant health consequences. Through community and regional planning that examines food quality and availability systemically, planners can play a significant role in shaping the food environment of communities, and thereby facilitate healthy eating. Drawing lessons from six case studies of communities nationwide, this report outlines strategies that planners can adopt to facilitate healthy eating through community and regional food planning.

That planners have a role to play in shaping food environments is anything but a new idea for the planning profession.

That planners have a role to play in shaping food environments is anything but a new idea for the planning profession. Beginning in the early 1900s, planners under various guises of regionalists, the City Beautiful Movement, and advocates of garden cities were discussing the role of cities and metropolitan regions and their governance and planning with regard to food (Donofrio 2007). This thread was essentially forgotten for decades. Re-emerging in the closing years of the century, planning scholars (Pothukuchi and Kaufman 2000) in the U.S. again began writing about planning's role in shaping the food system. They wondered why among the essential necessities of life —water, shelter, air, and food—planners had ignored food. The omission appeared especially puzzling because the food system is inherently affected by planning actions; traditional functional areas of planning, including transportation, economic development, and environment planning significantly affect people's ability to access food. Consider the following examples. Comprehensive plans and zoning codes regulate where food retail locates within a community. The availability of public transportation influences people's access to these retail outlets, especially for those who do not own personal automobiles. Of course, farmland preservation, a familiar planning preoccupation, directly influences the amount of land dedicated to farming, and, consequently, to food production. Despite these and many other critical connections between planning and food, until the late 1990s, food issues were largely a "stranger to the planning field" (Pothukuchi and Kaufman 2000).

Community and regional food planning—and planners' and local governments' involvement in it—has since come a long way. As this report documents, food planners and activists, working within the local government and nonprofit sectors, are engaged in community and regional food planning to promote healthy eating through a variety of programmatic, policy, and regulatory mechanisms. The American Planning Association too is taking an active role in this area. In 2005, APA sponsored the first ever track on food systems at its annual meeting. A year later, a volunteer Food Systems Steering Committee of APA members was established to "educate planners about food systems and to integrate food systems planning within traditional areas of planning" (www.planning.org/divisions/initiatives/foodsystem.htm). More recently, APA adopted a policy guide on community and regional food planning, signaling planners' commitment to actively engage in building and strengthening community food systems (www.planning.org/policy-guides/pdf/food.pdf). A key concern of this emerging area of community and regional food planning is the promotion of healthy eating.

Recent national trends have raised the salience of food and healthy eating as important topics. First, there is a growing public health concern over the rise in obesity. In response, a vast body of research and a number of programs to promote physical activity, and more recently to facilitate healthy eating, have emerged. The Robert Wood Johnson Foundation, a private philanthropic foundation, for example, dedicated millions of dollars toward programmatic initiatives, such as Active Living by Design, and its offshoot, Healthy Eating by Design (a sponsor of this report), to promote environmental and systemic solutions for promoting healthy eating and reducing obesity. Second, and related to the first, is a general increase in food activism and popular consciousness about where our food comes from and what we eat. The popularity of mainstream publications such as *Animal, Vegetable, Miracle* (Kingsolver 2007), *The Omnivore's Dilemma* (Pollan 2006) and *Fast Food Nation* (Schlosser 2001) illustrates this growing interest. And, finally, recent rising energy and food costs, which are making healthful foods less affordable to a wider swath of Americans, have catapulted food to the center of public debates in the country. Growing societal interests in issues of food and healthy eating make Kaufman and Pothukuchi's (2000) decade-old call to engage planners in improving the food system particularly prescient.

This PAS Report is a response to the growing interest in food and healthy eating among planners and communities nationwide. It describes how community and regional food planning can be used to facilitate healthy eating in communities. Following an introduction to community and regional food planning, this report describes survey results of planners' opinion of and role in this emerging area of planning. Because planners learn from practice, we provide case studies of six communities that have demonstrated leadership in promoting healthy eating using innovative strategies. The report concludes with strategies that planners can use to plan and design neighborhoods, routes, and destinations to facilitate healthy eating and build healthier communities.

WHAT IS COMMUNITY AND REGIONAL FOOD PLANNING?

Community and regional food planning is concerned with improving a community's food system. The term "food system" has been defined previously (Pothukuchi and Kaufman 2000) as the chain of activities and processes related to the production, processing, distribution, disposal, and eating of food. Food activists and scholars distinguish between a conventional and a community food system. Within a conventional food system, food production and processing is industrial in scale and relies on advances in bio-technology, food distribution occurs over large distances (estimates suggest food travels about 1,400 miles from the farm to the fork), disposal of food generates a significant amount of packaging waste, and consumers are removed— physically and metaphorically—from the source of their food. In such a system, corporations and agri-businesses, and not farmers, are dominant stakeholders. Government plays a role by providing significant subsidies to corporate producers and industrial farms for the production of specific crops, known as commodities, such as soy and corn. Scholars critique the conventional food system for its negative effect on the environment and economy of communities, as well as on public health.

A symptom of a malfunctioning food system is the absence of healthful food destinations within many neighborhoods in the U.S. A phrase commonly used to describe this inadequacy is a "food desert," or a neighborhood where few or no food stores are located. The term, originally coined in the United Kingdom, has a somewhat fluid and imprecise definition—some scholars use the phrase to refer to the absence of large supermarkets, while others use it to refer to the absence of supermarkets *and* smaller grocery stores. In any event, a significant body of literature is beginning to document racial and class disparities in access to particular types of food destinations, especially supermarkets (Raja et al. 2008; Mari Gallaghar Consulting and Research Group 2006). The implications of living in a food desert are many, especially for those without access to personal automobiles. Residents of food deserts may be unable to make frequent trips to distant food stores to purchase healthful foods. They may stock up on foods purchased during fewer trips, and may be less likely to purchase perishable fresh produce. If residents do buy fresh produce, the perishable nature of the food may lead to greater spoilage and wastage. Overall, limited access to healthful foods within the proximity of one's neighborhood may act as a barrier to eating healthy foods and have an adverse health impact on residents.

In contrast to a conventional food system, a community food system—favored by food system activists—emphasizes strengthening and making visible the relationships between producers, processors, distributors, and consumers of food. A community food system has several interrelated characteristics. It is place-based. The effort to promote local and regional

In contrast to a conventional food system, a community food system—favored by food system activists—emphasizes strengthening and making visible the relationships between producers, processors, distributors, and consumers of food.

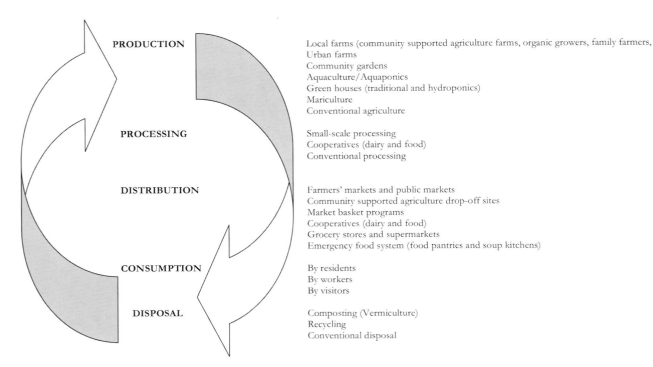

PRODUCTION	Local farms (community supported agriculture farms, organic growers, family farmers, Urban farms Community gardens Aquaculture/Aquaponics Green houses (traditional and hydroponics) Mariculture Conventional agriculture
PROCESSING	Small-scale processing Cooperatives (dairy and food) Conventional processing
DISTRIBUTION	Farmers' markets and public markets Community supported agriculture drop-off sites Market basket programs Cooperatives (dairy and food) Grocery stores and supermarkets Emergency food system (food pantries and soup kitchens)
CONSUMPTION	By residents By workers By visitors
DISPOSAL	Composting (Vermiculture) Recycling Conventional disposal

Figure 1-1. Components of a community's food system.

networks—among producers, processors, distributors, and consumers of food—is, therefore, considered desirable, and is in stark resistance to the conventional food system whose spatial scale frequently spans global proportions. A community food system promotes the use of environmentally sustainable methods for producing, processing, and distributing food. By favoring local distribution networks over global, the consumption of fossil fuel is minimized. In a similar vein, minimal packaging of food and composting of food leftovers is encouraged to reduce the impact on landfills. A community food system espouses the idea of social justice, placing at its center the concerns of marginalized groups, including migrant farm laborers, financially struggling family farmers, and underserved inner-city residents, rather than corporations and agri-businesses. And finally, and most pertinent to this report, a community food system facilitates residents' access to healthful, affordable, and culturally appropriate foods at all times—a condition described as "food security."

The need to re-strengthen community food systems is especially urgent in developing countries. In the absence of strong community food systems, the globalized food system defined by neoliberal policies imposed by entities such as the World Trade Organization and exploitative regulations imposed by food corporations make it difficult for developing nations to feed themselves. Scholar and activist Vandana Shiva (2000) notes that when corporations control the global food market, greater emphasis is placed on the production of fewer varieties of foods to ensure centralized control. Production of fewer varieties of crops reduces biodiversity: in Mexico, for example, about 80 percent of maize varieties are no longer available. To complicate matters, particular international trade treaties criminalize the traditional practice of seed saving and sharing by farmers in developing countries, limiting farmers' ability to grow foods and sustain themselves economically (Shiva 2000). Shiva argues that when "global markets replace local markets, monocultures replace diversity" in food supply and place developing countries at greater risk of environmental disaster and food insecurity.

Scholars caution planners to not equate local food systems with better food systems. Born and Purcell (2006) argue that there is nothing inherent about the local scale that makes local food systems better. Consider the following scenario. A doughnut manufacturing company is headquartered in city A; the company's retail outlets sell locally produced doughnuts in virtually every neighborhood in city A. By purchasing doughnuts at these retail outlets, residents of city A would be able to access and eat locally produced doughnuts; yet it would be a stretch to suggest that access to this locally produced food is better than apples trucked into the city from a different region. Born and Purcell (2006) suggest that community and regional food planners should first define the desired goals of a community food system—such as access to healthful, affordable, and nutritious food—and then determine the type and scale of food system that will help to achieve the desired goals. It is often the case that locally sourced products meet many of the desired goals of community food security better than globally sourced products.

Current Efforts to Promote Healthy Eating through Community and Regional Food Planning

Historically, planners and local governments have had a limited interest in food systems issues and food policy. Yet, thanks to the work and advocacy by a broad coalition of food system stakeholders, including local governments and planners, communities have made considerable strides in facilitating healthy eating by strengthening their community food systems. This chapter provides an overview of current efforts to promote healthy eating through community and regional food planning, giving special attention to the role of local governments and planners in facilitating such efforts.

Local governments are involved in a wide variety of efforts to strengthen food systems to facilitate healthy eating in their communities. Many provide resources to and facilitate the work of community food organizations, while others take a more active stance by establishing local and state food policy councils. In a few model cases, local governments have begun to explore the use of planning and regulatory mechanisms for promoting food security and facilitating healthy eating. For the sake of discussion, we classify these diverse approaches as programmatic, policy, and planning/regulatory efforts. This classification is not intended to be prescriptive, but it is intended as a heuristic device to organize and present the range of food-related efforts that are fast emerging.

Programmatic efforts refer to focused, often site-specific, programs, such as farmers' markets or summer meal programs for school children, which enhance access to healthful foods. Policy efforts are broader inasmuch as they seek to modify larger institutional, public, legal structures and policies to improve food systems and thereby facilitate healthy eating within a community. Planning and regulatory efforts make use of planning tools—such as comprehensive planning and zoning—for the same purpose. Below we describe each type of initiative and illustrate the description with examples from communities from across North America.

EXAMPLES OF PROGRAMMATIC EFFORTS

Community Gardens and Urban Farms

Community gardens are shared open spaces where individuals garden together to grow fresh, healthful, and affordable fruits and vegetables. Although community gardens are more common in urban neighborhoods, they can flourish in suburban settings as well. In addition to being productive spaces where people can grow affordable and healthful foods, community gardens provide numerous other benefits, many of which are much valued by planners. Like parks, they are lush green spaces that bring nature into a city, town, or village. Yet, unlike parks, which may be initiated and maintained by local governments, community gardens last only when there is community motivation, engagement, and ownership over the gardens. Community gardens function as civic spaces that promote social, cultural, and intergenerational exchange in a neighborhood. Many of these gardens exist within economically distressed neighborhoods, serving as icons of hope in these landscapes.

Figure 2-1. Hmong gardener in her community garden (Troy Garden) in Madison, Wisconsin.

Friends of Troy Gardens

The American Community Gardening Association estimates there are about 18,000 community gardens in the U.S. and Canada. Because many of them exist as informal spaces within a neighborhood, an accurate accounting of the total number of community gardens is nearly impossible. Nonetheless, their potential for increasing access to healthful foods is considerable, especially in low-income neighborhoods. In Ohio, for example, 337 urban gardens generated an annual harvest worth about $1 million (OSU 2000). Well over three-fourths (86 percent) of these gardens were used primarily to grow food for consumption (as opposed to flowers or other ornamental plants), while a small fraction (0.01 percent) were used to grow food for the market. On average, 44 percent of the food grown at these gardens was consumed by gardeners' immediate family members, another 20 percent was

Figure 2-2. Community garden in Buffalo, New York.

shared with other family members and friends, 13 percent was donated to food pantries, 20 percent was consumed on-site, and about 2 percent sold to grocery stores, restaurants, and other outlets (OSU 2000). Not only did these gardens increase access to fresh produce for the gardeners—three-fourths of whom identified themselves as low-income—but a considerable share of the produce made its way into the larger community through family, friends, and food pantries.

Gardeners recognize and enjoy the dietary benefits of having access to community gardens. For example, community gardeners surveyed in New Jersey reported improved nutrition as an important benefit of gardening. Forty-four percent of gardeners believed that they ate more fresh fruits and vegetables than nongardeners (Patel 1991). Youth gardeners in Buffalo also showed a demonstrable increase in consumption of fruits and vegetables after participation in a gardening program (Raja 2007).

More recently, community gardens and urban farms are gaining popularity as a local response to ameliorating the adverse effects of rising gas prices and climate change. By growing food locally using sustainable organic methods, community gardeners and urban farmers actively participate in reducing reliance on fossil fuels that would otherwise be necessary to grow and transport foods from long distances.

A large number of municipalities around the country support community gardens and urban agriculture. Cities lease land, provide water, compost, and even insurance to community gardens. In Buffalo, New York, for example, the city leases more than 30 publicly owned vacant lots for community gardens to Grassroots Gardens, a nonprofit group that acts as a liaison between the city and community gardeners and provides insurance to gardens. Many of these gardens also receive subsidized or free access to public infrastructure such as water supply and electricity. PAS Report 506/507, *Old Cities/Green Cities: Communities Transform Unmanaged Land*, documents the efforts of Philadelphia and the Pennsylvania Horticultural Society in turning that city's vacant land into a neighborhood resource, including a case study of the rebirth of the New Kensington Philadelphia neighborhood and a description of Philadelphia's Green City Strategy.

Lease agreements between municipalities and community groups for use of public land for community gardens can be fraught with tension when local governments perceive gardens as a temporary use of land, while gardeners see them as spaces vested with aspirations for their neighborhoods and countless hours of gardeners' sweat equity. This tension is especially pervasive in communities with booming real estate markets, where community gardens may be perceived by local governments as less than the "highest and best" use of land. Such tensions occasionally exist even in stagnant real estate markets. In Buffalo, the city can break its lease with Grassroots Gardens with a 30-day notice and reclaim ownership of community gardens located on publicly owned land. Melissa Fratello, former Grassroots Gardens' coordinator, notes that such breaks in leases occur not only in the face of the slightest development pressures but also when a mature community garden attracts the eye of entrepreneurial neighbors who bid to buy a "ready-made landscaped lot" from the city for a nominal charge.

While most community gardens programs are initiated and run by community groups, some local governments actively facilitate gardens within their neighborhoods. One of the most successful models is in Seattle, Washington, where a local government-run community gardening program has existed since the 1970s. The P-Patch program, housed in the city's Department of Neighborhoods, oversees the operation of more than 60 gardens throughout the city, with about 2,500 plots on 23 acres of publicly owned land (www.seattle.gov/neighborhoods/ppatch). While all citizens of Seattle are eligible to garden on these lots for a small fee, the program gives special consideration to low-income individuals, youth, and immigrants.

The City of Seattle provides ongoing administrative support to individuals and communities interested in establishing community gardens. The following is a sample of services offered by the Department of Neighborhoods' P-Patch program to residents interested in establishing a community garden:

- Evaluate potential of proposed garden site
- Help residents secure access to the land (through lease or purchase of public or privately owned land, including through the city's Neighborhood Matching Fund)
- Help with soil testing and recommend potential remediation techniques
- Lead a community group through a garden design process
- Manage plot assignment within the garden
- Monitor plots at each garden at least once a month to monitor plot usage and organic gardening, and work with site coordinators on issues that arise

- Maintain a waiting list for plots
- Attend to emergencies
- Facilitate outreach
- Provide materials and educational resources
- Facilitate dispute resolution in case of conflicts
- Develop and maintain interagency and outside organizational liaison

For almost four decades, P-Patch gardens have contributed to increasing access to healthful foods for Seattle's residents. About 6,000 people grow organic produce for consumption on these gardens. Gardeners are not allowed to sell the produce but are allowed to distribute it to friends, family, and food banks. Seven to 10 tons of organic produce is donated to food banks by P-Patch gardeners each year.

Community gardens offer a tremendous opportunity for people to grow and consume fresh, affordable, and healthful foods. This access is especially important for individuals with limited access to land and resources, such as renters who do not own land, and low-middle income populations who may wish to supplement their food budget by produce grown in the gardens.

Some cities, such as Goleta, California, Chicago, Illinois, and Madison, Wisconsin, are also home to functioning urban farms. In both Goleta and Madison, conservation easements protect urban farms from future development and ensure that residents have access to fresh fruits and vegetables. In some instances, cities have supported urban farming on land that would otherwise have been underused. For example, in Philadelphia, the Department of Community and Economic Development and the Philadelphia Water Authority facilitated the use of lands around a water tank site (the Somerton Tanks site in Northeast Philadelphia) as an economically sustainable urban farm. The Somerton Tanks Demonstration Farm had about half an acre of growing space and another quarter of an acre for pathways, parking, and farm structures. The farm, which started in 2003, generated $68,000 in its fourth year (2007) of operation.

In Chicago, Illinois, urban agriculture is moving center-stage into public parkland. Tucked in the middle of Grant Park, across from the path fronting Lake Michigan, is a beautifully designed "potager" or French kitchen garden with more than 150 varieties of vegetables, herbs, and edible flowers. The demonstration garden is the result of a partnership between Growing Power, a nonprofit organization headquartered in Milwaukee, and the Chicago Park and Recreation Department. The garden, designed and installed by Growing Power, produces about two tons of organic produce each growing season on about 20,000 square feet of growing area. Designers have paid special attention to the scale, texture, and color of the plants in the garden. As a result, the garden offers an excellent model for an aesthetically pleasing and edible landscape in a highly visible location in the city.

Farmers' Markets

Described as "recurrent markets at fixed locations where farm products are sold by farmers themselves" (Brown 2001), farmers' markets connect consumers to producers. The U.S. Department of Agriculture estimates that between 1994 and 2006, farmers' market grew in number from 1,755 to 4,385, a phenomenal increase over one decade (USDA 2007). At these farmers' markets, consumers can purchase fresh, locally grown, healthful produce from farmers. Occasionally, these markets also serve as retail venues for other goods, such as local handicrafts, baked goods, and other value-added food products. The presence of farmers' markets in cities, especially in low-income urban areas, presents an opportunity for both residents and farmers. Central-city neighborhoods often lack access to nutritious and fresh produce. For the same reason, these neighborhoods represent untapped markets for farmers.

Figure 2-3. Operating farmers markets in the United States.

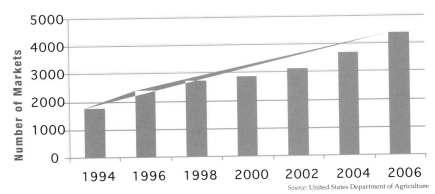

Source: United States Department of Agriculture

Developing a successful farmers' market requires more than simply inviting a group of farmers to drive their produce into a neighborhood, especially in a low-income neighborhood. Organizers have to choose a strategic site for their markets, such as areas of high foot traffic and near transit stops. Perhaps more importantly, farmers' markets have to respond to customers' economic realities in addition to their preferences and level of knowledge regarding healthful foods. In low-income neighborhoods, for example, farmers' markets may require initial assistance in the form of subsidies. They may also need to allow the use of food assistance vouchers such as from the Women and Infant Care (WIC) and the Seniors Farmers Markets Nutrition Programs (SFMNP). (See www.fns.usda.gov/wic/SeniorFMNP/SeniorFM-NPoverview.htm for more information.) To increase demand for the healthy food, farmers' markets in low-income neighborhoods may need to undertake education campaigns. Community organizing may also be necessary to develop a sense of ownership among both farmers and consumers. Market organizers must also consider potential language and cultural barriers that may prevent customers from participating in a farmers' market.

A farmers' market that manages to do the above and much more is the Fondy Farmers' Market in Northern Milwaukee, Wisconsin. The market was established in 2000 after an assessment of Milwaukee's food system in 1997 revealed that only a handful of supermarkets existed in the economically distressed areas of the central city (Kim 2008). Instead, corner convenience stores, with limited food offerings and prices as high as 30 percent more than suburban grocery stores, dominated the food environment.

Located on 38,000 square feet of city-owned land, Fondy Market operates six days a week during the growing season. Visitors and vendors at the market are protected from precipitation by a wood shelter built on the site in the 1970s. Somewhat ironically, the shelter was built to house a farmers' market that was eventually abandoned. The Fondy Food Center, the organization that oversees the market, leases the space (for 50 years) from the city for a dollar a year (Kim 2008).

At the Fondy Market, 35 farmers, many of whom are immigrants, sell an assortment of fresh fruits and vegetables. To ensure that low-income residents can make use of the market, Fondy accepts the Wisconsin QUEST Foodstamp Cards, only one of two markets in Wisconsin to do so. Farmers' markets were traditionally unable to use electronic benefit transfer (EBT) cards because these transactions require card readers with a telephone connection, which is not always available at market sites. At Fondy, farmers are able to accept food stamps using wireless handheld card readers.

A supply of healthful foods, while essential, may not be a sufficient strategy for facilitating healthy eating. To eat healthily, people must also have culinary and dietary education. Recognizing this, Fondy Markets' organizers run complementary nutrition education programs at the market. Through their Taste the Season workshops, area residents learn about nutrition, how to improve their cooking skills, and taste new foods. Audience members learn about, sample, and share new recipes featuring a different, locally grown, fresh vegetable that is in season and available at the market. Held every other Saturday throughout the market season, the workshops are conducted by a registered dietician and assisted by various culinary, nutrition, and health experts in the community. The organizers also raffle cookbooks and cooking utensils at these workshops (www. fondymarket.org/).

The creation of a farmers market is "a traditional, low-investment way" (fondymarket.org) to make fresh, healthful food available, to contribute to the vibrancy and vitality of a neighborhood, and to support the local farm economy.

Figure 2-3 (top). Neighborhood Across from Fondy Market, Milwaukee; Figure 2-5 (center). Fondy Farmers' Market in Milwaukee, Wisconsin; Figure 2-6 (below). Immigrant farmer at Fondy Farmers' Market.

In a CSA program, farmers sell shares of their upcoming harvest directly to consumers at the beginning of a growing season, bypassing intermediaries in the food retail chain between producers and consumers.

Community Supported Agriculture

Like farmers' markets, community supported agriculture (CSA) programs connect farmers directly with consumers. In a CSA program, farmers sell shares of their upcoming harvest directly to consumers at the beginning of a growing season, bypassing intermediaries in the food retail chain between producers and consumers. Shareholders receive shares of fresh produce weekly from the CSA farm and, in turn, share in the risks of farming, such as a poor harvest. Produce shares are delivered to shareholders at pre-arranged CSA drop-off sites by the farmer or volunteers.

Participation in a CSA ensures that city residents receive a steady supply of high-quality, fresh, typically organically grown produce during the growing season. CSAs reduce the distance over which food travels to reach the consumer. Transportation and storage costs are minimized. Thus, food sold through a CSA has the potential to be lower or comparable in cost to produce purchased at a conventional grocery store. CSA farms also typically use organic or more sustainable growing practices than conventional farms.

In addition to providing a steady supply of nutritious locally grown foods to consumers, a CSA arrangement also carries benefits for farmers. Primarily, it distributes risks across growers and consumers. It also provides farmers with capital at the beginning of the growing season, a time when farm expenses are high. A nationwide survey of CSA operators found that half of the farmers surveyed experienced an increase in their income after switching from conventional farming to community supported agriculture (Kelvin 1994).

Despite these benefits, CSAs programs have challenges to overcome. CSA consumers may feel that participation limits their choice of products (in comparison to purchasing the food at a conventional grocery store) since they generally receive only what is in season in their area, and some may lack the skills to cook the produce provided by the farmer. Successful CSA programs overcome this by providing information to consumers on the crops they are likely to receive over the growing season and by giving shareholders a recipe-of-the week for using the produce. Some CSAs, such as Full Circle Farms in Carnation, Washington, that serves the Puget Sound region, partner with other farming and natural foods producers and distributors to provide additional products not grown on the farm, including eggs, dairy, meat, juice, and fruit. This strategy raises question about the direct producer-consumer relationship for the CSA but certainly offers more convenience and variety to customers. Food distributed through CSAs may also be subject to a greater degree of wastage and spoilage if the amount that is delivered each week exceeds what they may be able to cook and consume.

CSAs also face special difficulties when serving low-income neighborhoods. CSAs require that consumers make one large payment for their share at the beginning of the growing season, or a few payments over the course of the season. Making these downpayments is not possible for residents on fixed income. Thus, even if the cost of produce from a CSA is lower or comparable to conventional produce, the purchase of shares at the beginning of the growing season can be cost prohibitive for some. However, CSAs have been creative in overcoming this challenge. Many offer a greater number of payments or smaller shares of produce to make the programs more appealing to customers. Some trade shares for on-farm picking and packing labor, or for delivery services. Yet other CSAs partner with nonprofit agencies that front the cost of shares for customers, and then recoup the costs over time from customers through pay-as-you-go programs. One innovative approach used in southern Wisconsin (home to many CSA farms) is a coalition of CSA farms (Madison Area Community Supported CSA farms: www.macsac.org) that addresses outreach and low-income share fundraising.

Farm-to-School Programs

Rates of obesity among youth nationwide have reached unprecedented levels. The CDC reports that the prevalence of overweight children between 6 and 11 years of age has more than doubled in the last two decades, from 7 percent in 1980 to 18.8 percent in 2004 (www.cdc.gov). The increase in overweight children is a significant health risk because it puts them at risk for other diseases, including diabetes. While a number of factors explain the prevalence of overweight children, the quality of foods available to them at home and school is an important one. One type of program that improves youth access to healthful foods is the farm-to-school program.

A farm-to-school program brings fresh, healthful foods from local farms to school cafeterias; these programs are designed to provide nutritional benefits to youth while expanding new market opportunities for farmers. Estimates from the Center for Food and Justice at Occidental College indicate a large number of communities have begun to establish farm-to-school programs: 38 states, 769 school districts, and 10,991 schools are currently operating 1,118 farm-to-school programs in the U.S.

Farm-to-School programs offer significant potential for improving food environments in schools, as well as for supporting the local farm economy.

In Buffalo, New York, such a farm-to-school program was piloted in 2006 in Bennett Park Montessori, a public school on the city's east side. Thirty-seven percent of the population in the school's surrounding neighborhood has an income below the poverty level, and 40 percent of the residents do not own a vehicle. The neighborhood contains a limited number of stores that sell fresh fruits, vegetables, and meats, creating a barrier to healthy eating (Raja and Breinlich 2007). The lack of car ownership combined with inadequate public transportation limit residents' ability to access healthful foods in this neighborhood. A local partnership of the school (its students, parents, teachers, and cafeteria staff), the school district, a nearby medical campus, a local farmer, and a local university, and several community groups led to the creation of a farm-to-school program at Bennett Park Montessori. Funded by the Healthy Eating by Design program of the Robert Wood Johnson Foundation, the farm-to-school program was part of a comprehensive effort by the local partnership to promote healthy eating among the school's youth through a variety of programs, including:

A farm-to-school program brings fresh, healthful foods from local farms to school cafeterias; these programs are designed to provide nutritional benefits to youth while expanding new market opportunities for farmers.

- a free weekly salad bar to serve local and organic produce free of charge to supplement the lunch in the school cafeteria for about 124 students, aged 11 to 13 years;

- after-school peer workshops to demonstrate growing, cooking, and consumption of healthy foods;

- integration of healthy eating concepts within the school's curriculum;

- reinforcement of healthy eating beyond the confines of the school day, such as by hosting dinners, featuring healthful and locally grown foods, for the families of students; and

- reinforcement of healthy eating concepts in the physical environment (e.g., students designed and created a portable mural depicting eating healthy in different growing seasons).

The implementation of a farm-to-school program is challenging. Local family farmers frequently lack the administrative capacity to meet the procurement guidelines of school districts, and they may not want to participate; local farms may be unable to supply sufficient produce to meet the demand of a large school district; and schools may lack resources and staff to implement a farm-to-cafeteria program. Cost is an important issue too because school districts are limited in how much they can spend per meal, and federal pass-through dollars for meal provision programs are insufficient, making cost-per-meal a potential barrier to implementation. As efficiencies increase with programmatic stabilization and understanding, this barrier will likely become less significant but not go away. This might require local purchasing agreements that go beyond lowest-cost bids to consider the multiple benefits that local farm purchasing can offer. Despite these challenges, farm-to-school programs hold significant promise from a planning perspective because they offer a mutually beneficial solution—one that facilitates healthy eating (for children) along with spurring economic development by redirecting public expenditures on school lunches to the local farm economy.

POLICY EFFORTS

While programs and projects to facilitate healthy eating are laudable, their replication and effectiveness is limited, and even hindered, by the absence of public policies that provide the governmental, legal, and institutional support for transforming community food systems. In recognition of this, a growing number of state and local governments are creating institutions and policies to strengthen food systems and facilitate healthy eating.

Food Policy Councils

A food policy council (FPC) is a group of individuals that advises local and state governments on matters related to food policy.[1] FPCs typically do not have the authority to pass laws, but they can be effective advocates for change within a local government. Food policy councils perform a variety of interrelated related tasks. They can:

- generate information on a community's food system, including commissioning and facilitating community food assessments;

- raise awareness of food issues within local government agencies and the public;

- develop food policy for government;

- advise on neighborhood, city, and regional comprehensive plans;

- develop guidelines for school nutrition programs;

- promote direct marketing opportunities such as institutional purchasing, farmers' markets, CSAs, and farm-to-institution programs;

- enhance existing program implementation, such as the Farmers' Market Nutrition Program, and Electronic Benefit Transfer card usage and participation;

- increase the effectiveness of existing food and hunger advocacy groups by developing partnerships and providing a forum for idea development and sharing;

- develop marketing initiatives to promote locally and sustainably grown foods; and

- organize regional conferences and national workshops to promote FPCs.

Members serving on FPCs may include or represent farmers, food processors, wholesalers, distributors, retailers, nutritionists, public health professionals, school food service staff, anti-hunger advocates, researchers, local government representatives, and concerned citizens (Borron 2003; Caton Campbell 2004). FPCs work closely with planning departments. In some instances, such as in Dane County, Wisconsin, FPCs are staffed by planners.

A food policy council (FPC) is a group of individuals that advises local and state governments on matters related to food policy.[1] FPCs typically do not have the authority to pass laws, but they can be effective advocates for change within a local government.

FPCs offer a community-driven, low-cost mechanism to assess and initiate food policy in a community.

The first FPC in the United States was established in Knoxville, Tennessee, in 1982. In the last decade, more than 35 FPCs at the local level (e.g., Kansas City, Kansas; Philadelphia; Portland, Oregon; Dane County, Wisconsin; Grand Rapids, Michigan) and state (e.g., Connecticut, Iowa, New Mexico, North Carolina, and Utah) have been created in the U.S. (APA 2007). There are now approximately 70 nationwide at different levels of formation and authority. Two important FPCs are briefly described below; readers are also encouraged to learn about them through their websites, which we offer in the descriptions.

Portland, Oregon. The Portland-Multnomah Food Policy Council (PMFPC) gathers and disseminates information on food-related issues, advising both Portland and Multnomah County governments. It also advocates for local government initiatives that strengthen community and regional food systems. Their Diggable City project, for example, resulted in the development of a citywide database that identifies lands suitable for food production. As a result of PMFPC's work, in 2005, the Portland City Council approved funding for a full-time staff position (a "food planner") to work in the Office of Sustainable Development. This staff person now works with the FPC to develop recommendations about food access, local food purchasing plans, and other community and regional food-planning initiatives (www.portlandonline.com/osd). Additional information on the Portland-Multnomah Food Policy Council is available in the case study section.

Toronto, Canada. Toronto has a distinguished history of food policy making. Lacking federal and provincial leadership on food security issues, in 1991 the city created the Toronto Food Policy Council (TFPC) as a subcommittee of the Toronto Board of Health. The TFPC mission is:

> [To partner] with business and community groups to develop policies and programs promoting food security. Our aim is a food system that fosters equitable food access, nutrition, community development and environmental health.

Like most FPCs, the Toronto Food Policy Council has no authority to pass or enforce laws. Yet the council has successfully advocated and implemented a number of food-related policies. A few of these are listed below; for a complete listing see the TFPC website (www.toronto.ca/health/tfpc_index.htm).

- Contributed text on food issues for inclusion in the City of Toronto's official plan
- Authored and advocated for the City of Toronto Food and Nutrition Declaration in 1991
- Networked with city agencies to develop strategies to improve Toronto's food system
- Participated in raising approximately 3.5 million dollars for food projects
- Designed and administered the City's Food Access Grants program, which distributed 2.4 million dollars toward purchase of kitchen equipment for 180 schools and social service agencies
- Advocated for and facilitated institutional purchasing of locally produced food by eight hospitals in the Ontario region

Recognizing the interdisciplinary nature of food issues, the Council sees itself as "a forum for discussing and integrating policy issues that often fall between the cracks of established departments and research specialties" (www.toronto.ca/health/tfpc_index.htm).

The first FPC in the United States was established in Knoxville, Tennessee, in 1982. In the last decade, more than 35 FPCs at the local level have been created in the U.S.

Food Charters

A food charter is a statement of vision, values, and principles to guide a community's food system. Several cities, mostly in Canada, have adopted food charters. These include Toronto, Saskatoon, Manitoba, and, most recently, Vancouver. In many instances, the food charters are crafted and adopted in large part due to the work and advocacy of food policy councils.

Toronto, Ontario. Facilitated by the Toronto Food Policy Council, in 2001, Toronto's city council voted unanimously to adopt a food charter. Toronto's Food Charter is a holistic approach to food security for all Torontonians in an effort to contribute to the health and well-being of city residents. An excerpt from the charter is shown in Figure 2-7. The charter cites 10 reasons why the city chooses to ensure food security:

1. Food security means no one in the city goes to bed hungry.

2. Food security makes the city more affordable.

3. Food security means every child gets a head start.

4. Food security saves on medical care.

Figure 2-7. Excerpt from Toronto's Food Charter.

Toronto's Food Charter

In 1976, Canada signed the United Nations Covenant on Social, Economic and Cultural Rights, which includes "the fundamental right of everyone to be free from hunger." The City of Toronto supports our national commitment to food security, and the following beliefs:

Every Toronto resident should have access to an adequate supply of nutritious, affordable and culturally-appropriate food.

Food security contributes to the health and well-being of residents while reducing their need for medical care.

Food is central to Toronto's economy, and the commitment to food security can strengthen the food sector's growth and development.

Food brings people together in celebrations of community and diversity and is an important part of the city's culture.

Therefore, to promote food security, Toronto City Council will:

- champion the right of all residents to adequate amounts of safe, nutritious, culturally-acceptable food without the need to resort to emergency food providers
- advocate for income, employment, housing, and transportation policies that support secure and dignified access to the food people need
- support events highlighting the city's diverse and multicultural food traditions
- promote food safety programs and services
- sponsor nutrition programs and services that promote healthy growth and help prevent diet-related diseases
- ensure convenient access to an affordable range of healthy foods in city facilities
- adopt food purchasing practices that serve as a model of health, social and environmental responsibility

- partner with community, cooperative, business and government organizations to increase the availability of healthy foods
- encourage community gardens that increase food self-reliance, improve fitness, contribute to a cleaner environment, and enhance community development
- protect local agricultural lands and support urban agriculture
- encourage the recycling of organic materials that nurture soil fertility
- foster a civic culture that inspires all Toronto residents and all city departments to support food programs that provide cultural, social, economic and health benefits
- work with community agencies, residents' groups, businesses and other levels of government to achieve these goals.

 TORONTO

5. Food security means more local jobs.

6. Food security is environmentally friendly.

7. Food security reduces traffic pollution.

8. Food security is good business.

9. Food security means waste not, want not.

10. Food security is neighbourly. (Toronto Food Charter 2001)

Vancouver, British Columbia. Guided by a sustainability framework, the Vancouver City Council voted to adopt a food charter in February 2007. Similar to the TFPC, the Vancouver Food Charter presents a vision for a food system that benefits the community and environment (Figure 2-8). The charter uses five guiding principles to reach its vision: community economic development, ecological health, social justice, collaboration and participation, and celebration (Vancouver Food Charter 2007). The charter provides a list of action steps that support the vision of the Charter, including the following:

- Improve access to healthy and affordable foods

- Support regional farmers and food producers

- Expand urban agriculture and food recovery operations

- Increase the health of all members of the city

- Celebrate our city's diverse food cultures

VANCOUVER FOOD CHARTER
January 2007

The Vancouver Food Charter presents a vision for a food system which benefits our community and the environment. It sets out the City of Vancouver's commitment to the development of a coordinated municipal food policy, and animates our community's engagement and participation in conversations and actions related to food security in Vancouver.

VISION

The City of Vancouver is committed to a just and sustainable food system that

- contributes to the economic, ecological, and social well-being of our city and region;
- encourages personal, business and government food practices that foster local production and protect our natural and human resources;
- recognizes access to safe, sufficient, culturally appropriate and nutritious food as a basic human right for all Vancouver residents;
- reflects the dialogue between the community, government, and all sectors of the food system;
- celebrates Vancouver's multicultural food traditions.

PREAMBLE

In a food-secure community, the growing, processing and distribution of healthy, safe food is economically viable, socially just, environmentally sustainable and regionally based.

Some members of our community, particularly children, do not have reliable access to safe and nutritious food. In addition, much of the food we eat travels long distances from where it is grown and processed and is dependent on fossil fuels at every stage. Dependency on imports for our food increases our impact on the environment and our vulnerability to food shortages from natural disasters or economic set-backs. Overall food security is increasingly influenced by global factors that affect our community's ability to meet our food system goals.

Community food security needs the involvement of all members of our community, including citizens, consumers, businesses and governments. When citizens are engaged in dialogue and action around food security, and governments are responsive to their communities' concerns and recommendations, sound food policy can be developed and implemented in all sectors of the food system and the community.

In 2002, the City of Vancouver adopted sustainability as a fundamental approach for all the City's operations. The goal of a just and sustainable food system plays a significant role in achieving a "Sustainable Vancouver".

Figure 2-8. Excerpt from Vancouver's Food Charter.

School Food Policy

As noted above, the prevalence of youth obesity has emerged as a significant public health concern in the U.S. Because children spend a significant amount of their day in schools, there is renewed focus on the impact of school environments on obesity and children's health in general. School districts and schools are considering and creating comprehensive school food policies to facilitate healthy eating, physical activity, and overall healthy lifestyles for children within the school environment. An extra boost to school food policy making came in 2004 when, as part of the Child Nutrition and WIC Reauthorization, the federal government mandated all school districts receiving federal funds for meal programs to create school wellness policies by the start of 2006-2007 school year (Child Nutrition and WIC Reauthorization Act of 2004; S.2507); the Act requires that schools have a wellness policy that:

1. includes goals for nutrition education, physical activity, and other school based activities that are designed to promote student wellness in a manner that the local educational agency determines is appropriate;

2. includes nutrition guidelines selected by the local educational agency for all foods available on each school campus under the local educational agency during the school day with the objectives of promoting student health and reducing childhood obesity;

3. provides an assurance that guidelines for reimbursable school meals shall not be less restrictive than regulations and guidance issued by the Secretary of Agriculture pursuant to subsections (a) and (b) of section 10 of the Child Nutrition Act (42 U.S.C. 1779) and sections 9(f)(1) and 17(a) of the Richard B. Russell National School Lunch Act (42 U.S.C. 1758(f)(1), 1766(a)), as those regulations and guidance apply to schools;

4. establishes a plan for measuring implementation of the local wellness policy, including designation of 1 or more persons within the local educational agency or at each school, as appropriate, charged with operational responsibility for ensuring that the school meets the local wellness policy; and

5. involves parents, students, representatives of the school food authority, the school board, school administrators, and the public in the development of the school wellness policy.

Madison, Wisconsin. In July 2006, the Madison Metropolitan School District (MMSD) adopted a Food Policy as part of the district's overall Wellness Policy. The Food Policy contains numerous guidelines to create a school environment that encourages healthful eating. According to MMSD, the school district's policy requires the following:

- Schools shall provide nutrition education and physical education to foster lifelong habits of healthy eating and physical activity, and shall establish linkages between health education and school meal programs, and other activities that occur within the school day.

- All students in grades K-12 shall have opportunities and encouragement to be physically active on a regular basis.

- Foods and beverages sold or served at school during the school day, at school sponsored events and in MSCR [the Madison School-Community Recreation department] programs for students shall meet the nutrition recommendations of the U.S. Dietary Guidelines for Americans, 2005.

- To the maximum extent practicable, all schools in the MMSD shall participate in available federal school meal programs.

Like school food policy initiatives in other communities, MMSD's food policy was the result of collaborative work by numerous food system stakeholder groups, including the Wisconsin Homegrown Lunch project of the Research, Education, Action, and Policy Food Group (REAP), and the University of Wisconsin's Center for Integrated Agricultural Systems.

Among all the food policy initiatives described in this PAS Report, planners are perhaps least involved in school food policy. While planners' distance from schools' internal programming and policy making is understandable, planning and school food policy may intersect. Consider the following example. In Seattle, Washington, following the passage of a strict school nutrition policy, students at Cleveland High school started going off campus to purchase junk foods from nearby convenience and grocery stores (*Seattle*

Times, December 19, 2006). The location of convenience stores and fast-food restaurants near schools, regulated to some degree by land-use planning and zoning, facilitates children's access to less healthful foods and works at odds with the school district's wellness policy. Thus, while planners may not have a direct impact on internal school food environments, planners' work in the surrounding community may affect student food access.

PLANNING AND ZONING

Local governments and planners have begun to deploy traditional—and nontraditional—planning and regulatory mechanisms to improve food environments to facilitate healthy eating. Some communities that use community and regional food planning to facilitate healthy eating are Marin County and Benicia, California; Madison and Milwaukee, Wisconsin; and Waterloo, Ontario, and Vancouver, British Columbia (Glosser et al. 2007).

Stand-alone Plans Focusing on Community Food Systems or Their Components

Relative to other areas of planning, community and regional food planning is relatively new. As such, there are few stand-alone municipally sponsored and adopted plans that deal exclusively with community food systems or with an element of community food systems. Nonetheless, there are a few examples (Waterloo, Ontario; Oakland, California; and Madison, Wisconsin) where local and regional governments have authored or have been involved in plans dealing with the food system in its entirety or with an element of it. These plans offer a useful template for communities considering the creation of stand-alone and comprehensive food system plans.

The Waterloo, Ontario, food system plan. In April 2007, the public health department of the Regional Municipality of Waterloo, Ontario, published a food systems plan, "A Healthy Community Food System Plan for the Waterloo Region." The plan's goal is to create a system in which all residents of Waterloo Region have access to (and can afford to buy) safe, nutritious, and culturally acceptable food produced in a way that sustains the environment and rural communities (Meidema and Pigott 2007). It outlines a series of objectives and strategies for meeting this goal, as shown in Figure 2-9. Based

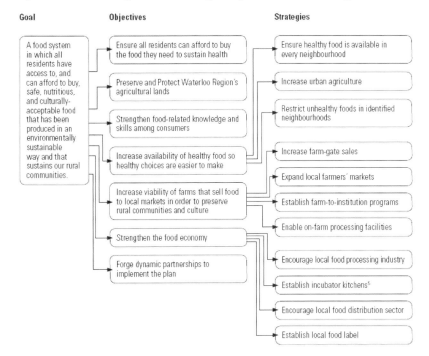

Figure 2-9. Excerpt from Waterloo Region's Food System Plan.

Inclusion of food issues in a comprehensive plan ensures that, along with ensuring adequate housing, jobs, transportation, etc., a community is positioned to have a well-functioning community food system in the future—one that provides access to healthful and affordable foods for all residents.

on information collected through a series of focus groups, the plan, which was developed within a public health agency whose staff includes a land-use planner, makes several recommendations for municipal and township planners. Key recommendations include increasing availability of healthful foods in all neighborhoods and limiting unhealthful foods within identified neighborhoods through zoning. The plan notes that the first recommendation received considerable support from focus group participants, while the latter received a somewhat mixed response. Implementing the plan's recommendations faces regulatory challenges, an aspect we discuss below in the section on zoning and regulation.

Oakland, California, Resoloution 79680. In January 2006, the Oakland City Council Life Enrichment Committee unanimously passed a resolution (#79680) authorizing "the Mayor's Office of Sustainability to develop an Oakland Food Policy and Plan for thirty percent local area food production, by undertaking an initial food system assessment study."

The plan's goals included: maximizing food security; promoting urban agriculture and waste reduction, economic development, and agricultural preservation; and enhancing food literacy and capacity among residents to make healthful and sustainable food choices. Following the plan's completion, the city passed a resolution to implement the plan's key recommendations to create a citywide food policy council. To facilitate this, the city passed a Request for Proposals (RFP) to contract with an organization to develop the best strategy for establishing a FPC. The city allocated $50,000 as start-up funds toward the creation of the FPC.

The Madison, Wisconsin, Community Gardens Plan. In 1999, the Community Gardens Advisory Committee of the City of Madison adopted an action plan to create and sustain community gardens (Raja 2000). Recommendations arising from this action plan were subsequently incorporated into the 2006 Comprehensive Plan for the City of Madison (City of Madison Comprehensive Plan 2006). Additional details on how the recommendations of the community gardens plan were adopted into Madison's Comprehensive Plan are provided in a case study in Chapter 4.

Inclusion of Food System Components in Comprehensive Plans

Comprehensive plans provide a roadmap for the future growth of a community. Inclusion of food issues in a comprehensive plan ensures that, along with ensuring adequate housing, jobs, transportation, etc., a community is positioned to have a well-functioning community food system in the future—one that provides access to healthful and affordable foods for all residents. A number of local and regional governments in the U.S. and Canada, from Benicia, California, to Toronto, Ontario, recognize the key role of comprehensive plans in ensuring a food secure future for its residents. Brief descriptions of the Benicia and Marin County, California; Seattle, Washington; and Madison, Wisconsin, programs follow.

Benicia, California. Benicia included policies to promote healthy eating in its 2003 comprehensive plan update. The Community Health and Safety chapter supports the creation of demonstration gardens and recommends using vacant property for fruit and vegetable gardening.

Marin County, California. On the West Coast, Marin County has emerged as a leader in the area of rural food planning, having recently included a community food component within the natural resource element of their latest countywide comprehensive plan. Additional details are provided in a case study of Marin County in Chapter 4.

Seattle, Washington. In large part due to the success of P-Patch program (described above), Seattle's Comprehensive Plan pays significant attention to community gardens as a source of healthful foods within a neighborhood. The plan, originally adopted in 1994 and subsequently updated in 2005, calls for one community garden for each 2,000 households in its urban village or areas "where conditions can best support increased density needed to house and employ the city's newest residents" (City of Seattle Comprehensive Plan 2005, p 1.3). Section UVG40 of the 2005 update of the Comprehensive Plan calls for the provision of connections linking urban centers to community gardens and recommends the acquisition of property for community gardens as part of the open space acquisition plan.

Madison, Wisconsin. Owing to a broad coalition between city and county governments, citizen groups, and the local university, the City of Madison's 2006 Comprehensive Plan includes a significant section on food. The recommendations of the plan range from creation of community gardens to supporting the countywide food council. Details on Madison's efforts are provided in Chapter 4.

Zoning with Food and Health in Mind

Zoning is an artifact of planning's deep historic links with public health concerns. Drawing on the legal authority of the police power vested in states or their designated local governments, zoning emerged to regulate land development to protect the health, welfare, and overall well-being of a society. The contemporary application of zoning, however, is largely driven by considerations other than health; these considerations include the degree to which a proposed use will fit the character of a community or the amount of traffic it will generate, etc. Nonetheless, zoning is almost always invoked in the name of public health and welfare. Given recent concerns over "food deserts" and obesity, there is a great deal of interest—and debate—regarding the use of zoning to facilitate public health, especially by regulating the presence of particular types of foods destinations in a community.

How are communities using zoning and city ordinances to regulate food destinations? The use of zoning codes and municipal ordinances to facilitate food destinations varies widely. Ordinances frequently invoke the idea of public health, although the concerns noted pertain to sanitation, cleanliness, and contamination, perhaps reflecting the concerns of a past era when these were the most pressing public health concerns. Consider the following example of Buffalo, New York.

Buffalo, New York. The city ordinance in Buffalo, New York, regulates fruits and vegetable vendors as follows:

> Every person, firm or corporation operating any premises [namely, outdoor shops, stands, or markets selling fruits and vegetables] in said City under a license as herein provided...shall not permit or allow any diseased, rotten or decayed fruits, vegetables or substance to be offered for sale or to remain upon said premises. (Charter and code of the City of Buffalo, Article 199-4)

Also motivated by similar concerns, the ordinance also stipulates the following regarding wholesale fruit and vegetable sellers:

> It shall be unlawful for any itinerant wholesale dealer in fruits and vegetables to sell or to have in his possession with the intention of selling or offering for sale any of the merchandise mentioned in this article which is unclean, unwholesome, tainted, putrid, decayed, poisoned or in any manner rendered unsafe or unwholesome for human consumption. Such merchandise shall be deemed unwholesome for human food if the same has been contaminated by flies or other insects, vermin, dust, dirt or other foreign contamination or if said merchandise contains any poisonous or deleterious or injurious ingredients in kind and quantities so as to render such merchandise injurious or detrimental to health. (Charter and code of the City of Buffalo, Article 199-14)

Given recent concerns over "food deserts" and obesity, there is a great deal of interest—and debate—regarding the use of zoning to facilitate public health, especially by regulating the presence of particular types of foods destinations in a community.

In the U.S. currently, the lack of sanitation related to the production of fresh produce and vegetables is arguably a lesser public health concern than the complete absence of fresh produce and vegetables, especially in low-income neighborhoods predominantly served by food retailers that sell foods high in calories and low in nutrients (e.g., fast-food restaurants).

Some municipalities do use zoning codes to limit the presence of food venues that may have a detrimental public health impact—namely, fast-food destinations. Consider the following example from Concord, Massachusetts.

Concord, Massachusetts. In Concord, the town's zoning law imposes an outright ban on fast-food restaurants (Town of Concord, Massachusetts, Zoning Bylaws, section 4.7.1, p.18). It stipulates:

> Drive-in or fast food restaurants are expressly prohibited. A drive-in or fast-food restaurant is defined as any establishment whose principal business is the sale of foods or beverages in a ready-to-consume state, for consumption within the building or off-premises, and whose principal method of operation includes: (1) sale of foods and beverages in paper, plastic or other disposable containers; or (2) service of food and beverages directly to a customer in a motor vehicle.

In the case of Concord and a number of other municipalities, the ban on fast-food restaurants is generally not invoked in the name of public health; instead, it is invoked in the name of protection of community character, aesthetic reasons, or preventing traffic problems. In some cases, however, the zoning code has been used to regulate fast-food restaurants for reasons of public health, as noted in the following two cases.

Arcata, California. In 2001, Arcata's Democracy and Corporations Committee formed a subcommittee to research ordinances on fast-food jurisdictions for reasons of better protecting the public health. The city held four public hearings on the issue, and approximately 75 percent of the residents voiced their support in favor of an ordinance to limit "formula restaurants" (see definition below) (www.worldhungeryear.com). In 2002, Arcata's common council enacted an ordinance to modify the city's zoning ordinance to limit formula restaurants within city limits due to reasons of "public health, safety, and general welfare" (City of Arcata, Ordinance no.1333).

Ordinance 1333 defines formula restaurants as follows:

> A retail establishment primarily devoted to the on-site preparation and offering of food and beverage for sale to the public for consumption either on or off the premises and which is required by contractual or other arrangement to offer any of the following: standardized menus, ingredients, food preparation, decor, uniforms, architecture, signs or similar standardized features and which causes it to be substantially identical to more than eleven (11) other restaurants regardless of ownership or location.

Ordinance 1333 limits formula restaurants in the commercial and industrial zone districts in the city to nine (the number in the city at the time the ordinance was enacted). Specifically, the ordinance notes:

> The number of Formula Restaurants in Arcata shall be limited to nine (9) establishments from the date of the adoption of this ordinance. A new Formula Restaurant shall only be allowed if it replaces an existing Formula Restaurant in one of the following business districts: Janes Road [1], Northtown [1], Uniontown [2], and Valley West/Giuntoli Lane [5]. The allowed number of Formula Restaurants per business district has been indicated in the brackets, and replacement Formula Restaurants are allowed within the business district boundaries as identified in Attachment 1. All other business districts, as labeled in Attachment 1, shall not allow Formula Restaurants.

Although the ordinance initially generated opposition from local franchise owners, the opposition eventually subsided since the ordinance allowed

In the U.S. currently, the lack of sanitation related to the production of fresh produce and vegetables is arguably a lesser public health concern than the complete absence of fresh produce and vegetables.

existing establishments to dominate the local formula restaurant market (www.worldhungeryear.com). Other municipalities, such as Los Angeles and New York (Fernandez 2006; City of Los Angeles Press Release 2007), are also examining similar restrictions owing to reasons of public health, although formal zoning changes have not yet been adopted.

Los Angeles. On Dec 11, 2007, the Los Angeles City Council Planning and Land Use Management Committee (PLUM) approved an Interim Control Ordinance (ICO) to limit new fast-food restaurants.

The ordinance proposes a one-year period during which new fast-food establishments will not be allowed to open in the South Los Angeles, Southeast Los Angeles, West Adams, Baldwin Hills and Leimert Park community planning areas. This will allow time for city planners to study the economic and environmental effects of the proliferation of fast-food restaurants in these communities and develop permanent solutions.

As noted above, in most cases (except the ban in Arcata and the moratorium in Los Angeles), zoning limits on fast-food restaurants are generally invoked on the basis of these establishments' negative impact on aesthetic quality, traffic levels, or overall character of the community. However, legal scholars (Mair et al. 2005) argue that zoning limits on fast-food restaurants are as, if not more, likely to be upheld by the courts for reasons of poor nutritional quality of foods because this has a more direct impact on the health and welfare of the public.

In some instances, zoning codes can act as barriers to businesses that bring healthful foods into neighborhoods. In these cases, communities have used creative strategies to overcome these barriers, as noted in the example from Kitchener.

Kitchener, Ontario. Following the recommendations of its food system plan, the Waterloo Public Health agency, along with several partners, recently initiated an implementation effort to start neighborhood produce markets in underserved areas in the city of Kitchener. However, the concept of a neighborhood produce market did not fit neatly into the city's regulatory framework. An evaluation report by the Waterloo Region Public Health agency notes:

> Local farmers, if they wish to sell their produce directly to the public outside of designated farmers' market areas, need to follow a licensing process that differs from those at farmers' markets. Each municipality has a unique license fee for outdoor vendors who wish to sell their wares (e.g. flowers, hot dogs) however there is no by-law or license for vendors wishing to sell fruits and vegetables outside of farmers' markets. If these produce vendors were to be "accommodated" under the hot dog vendor license then each vendor would need to buy a license and be 200 meters apart from one another. (Miedima 2008)

In essence, the regulatory framework is a barrier to the creation of neighborhood markets. The partnership leading the neighborhood market effort devised a novel way to work around this barrier.

> As a solution to this problem, the idea of having several farmer vendors at one market was abandoned for the 2007 season. Instead—following the community collaboration model—Opportunities Waterloo Region and the Highland Stirling Community Group applied for vendor licenses to sell locally grown fruits and vegetables that were bought from various local farmers. (Miedima 2008)

Eventually, Kitchener also ruled that a variance would not be required for these neighborhood markets under the existing zoning law because the markets served a public interest. Therefore, the markets would be considered a permitted use.

Legal scholars (Mair et al. 2005) argue that zoning limits on fast-food restaurants are as, if not more, likely to be upheld by the courts for reasons of poor nutritional quality of foods because this has a more direct impact on the health and welfare of the public.

The lesson for other jurisdictions is that implementation will almost inevitably reveal ambiguity or inadequacy in regulatory tools. Jurisdictions need to both understand this and be prepared for flexibility or amendments to such new tools.

In some cases, local governments have begun to use zoning codes to facilitate access to healthful foods, such as in Milwaukee.

Milwaukee, Wisconsin. In Milwaukee, the zoning ordinance was amended in 2005 to permit agricultural uses, such as greenhouses and the raising of crops, in all residential and zoning districts. The zoning ordinance was also amended to authorize the cultivation of crops in park districts (Glosser et al. 2007).

For zoning modifications to be effective and legally defensible in facilitating access to healthful foods or in limiting access to unhealthful foods, it is important that they be informed by a thorough food assessment and food planning process.

CHAPTER 3

A Nationwide Survey of Planners About Promoting Healthy Eating Through Planning

Community and regional food planning is gathering momentum nationwide. In this dynamic period, we asked planners their opinion about their role in facilitating healthy eating through community and regional food planning. To answer this question, the authors conducted an on-line survey of APA members from September 2007 to January 2008.

The survey was designed to partially follow up on Kaufman and Pothukuchi's (2000) survey conducted in 1996-97.[2] One-hundred and ninety-two APA members responded to this survey.[3] Respondents represented a broad cross section of APA membership. A significant percentage are currently involved in land-use planning (20 percent), comprehensive planning (14 percent), community development (14 percent), environmental planning (11 percent), and transportation planning (10 percent), while the remaining are affiliated with a variety of other areas of planning, including a small group of four (2.5 percent) who identified themselves as working primarily in the area of community and regional food planning (Figure 3-1). The respondents represent a wide swath of planning organizations: A majority (57 percent) work for the government sector, while about a quarter (23 percent) work for private consulting organizations, while the remaining work for nonprofit organizations, law firms, development firms, and research organizations. About 45 percent of the respondents are certified by the American Institute of Certified Planners (AICP), and about 60 percent of the respondents had a graduate degree in planning. A majority (57 percent) were female.

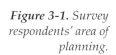

Figure 3-1. Survey respondents' area of planning.

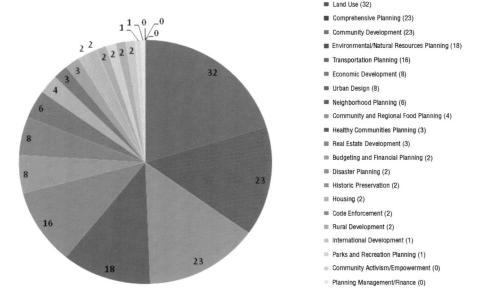

PLANNERS' OPINIONS ABOUT THE PROFESSION'S INVOLVEMENT IN FOOD AND HEALTHY EATING ISSUES

Respondents were asked to rank the level of involvement from 1 (no involvement) to 5 (top priority) that the profession of planning should have in a number of food-related issues. The list of key food issues and their ranking is shown in Figure 3-2.[4] Results from the survey indicate widespread support for the planning involvement in food and healthy eating issues: a majority of respondents cited food and healthy eating issues as a "significant" or "top" priority.

Planning for farmland preservation elicited the greatest support from respondents. About 90 percent of respondents were of the opinion that farmland preservation should be a significant or top priority for the planning profession. This is in spite of the fact that only 42 percent of the respondents' work was in a rural setting. This resounding support for this issue is not surprising given that planners have long grappled with the issue of farmland preservation (and sprawl, which is seen as a threat to farmland preservation). Respondents also ranked promoting food access using public transportation and planning mixed-use development to include food destinations as areas of significant or top priority for planning.

Interestingly, considerable support exists among APA members to support food and healthy eating efforts using traditional planning tools, such as comprehensive planning, neighborhood planning, and zoning. About 70 percent of respondents believed that the preparation and modification of comprehensive plans to include community and regional food issues should be an area in which the planning profession should be significantly involved, while a slightly higher percentage (73 percent) felt the same way about preparation or modification of zoning codes to regulate location of food retail. This support is a remarkable shift from even a decade ago. In 1997-1998, for example, a survey of planners from 22 cities reported that only 38 percent of planners agreed that "planners should get more involved in food system planning in the future" (Pothukuchi and Kaufman 2000). Overall, the results of this survey clearly point to a growing recognition and support for food and healthy eating issues among APA members.

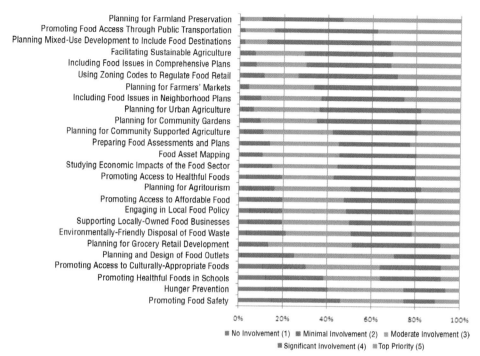

Figure 3-2. *Preference for the planning profession's involvement in food and healthy eating issues.*

PLANNING ORGANIZATIONS' INVOLVEMENT IN PLANNING FOR HEALTHFUL FOOD ACCESS AND HEALTHY EATING

Despite their preferences to be involved, 71 percent of APA members who took the survey report that their planning organizations have no or minimal involvement in food and healthy eating issues (Figure 3-3). Upon probing members' responses regarding their organizations' involvement in particular food issues (e.g., community gardening, farmland preservation, etc.), the answers painted a more complex picture. Perhaps not surprisingly, 60 percent of all organizations have a significant involvement in farmland preservation activities, a food-related area familiar to planners; on the other hand, 50 percent of all organizations are significantly involved in promoting mixed-use development that includes food destinations.

Plan-making, the core activity of planners, is beginning to incorporate food issues as well. Twenty-two percent of APA members report that their planning organizations are at least "moderately involved" in preparing or modifying comprehensive plans to include issues related to food. In fact, the 2008 APA National Planning Excellence Award for Implementation was awarded to a countywide plan that includes food as a component of the agriculture and natural resource element of the plan. (See the full case study of this award winner, the Marin Countywide Plan, in Chapter 4.)

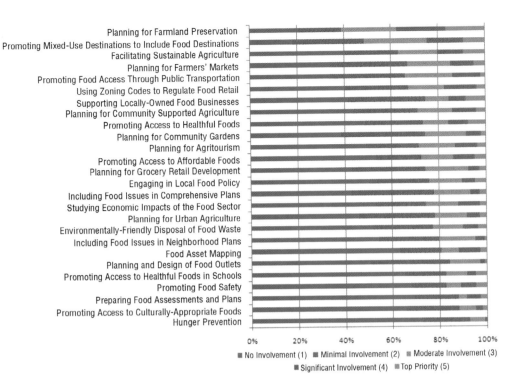

Figure 3-3. Planning organizations' involvement in food and healthy eating issues.

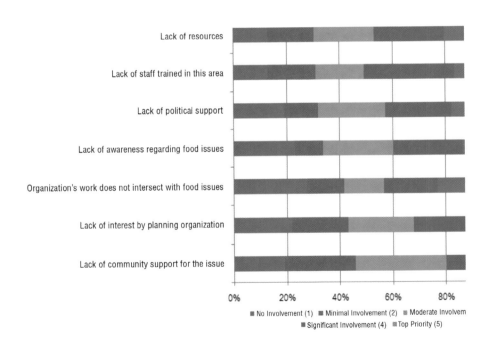

Figure 3-4. Barriers to planning organizations' involvement in food and healthy eating issues.

Planning organizations are also involved in food issues through regulatory mechanisms, such as zoning. In fact, about a third of planning organizations are involved in using zoning codes to regulate food retail. Whether these regulations facilitate healthy eating choices is not possible to tell from this survey, but it is clear that planners have a hand in shaping food environments of communities.

Despite the involvement of planning organizations in food issues, it is quite clear that a significant gap exists between planners' preferred level of involvement in the area of food systems and their planning organizations' actual involvement. In the next section we explore the possible explanations for this gap.

MAJOR BARRIERS TO PLANNING ORGANIZATIONS' INVOLVEMENT IN PROMOTING ACCESS TO HEALTHFUL FOODS

A number of interrelated factors explain planning organizations involvement in food issues. Figure 3-4 shows a list of factors ranked by APA members as possible explanations. When ranked in order of their importance, where 1 stood for a "not at all important" explanation, and 5 stood for "a primary explanation" for their organizations' lack of involvement, APA members ranked explanations as follows: lack of resources (3.25), lack of trained staff (3.24), lack of political support (3.11), lack of organizational awareness (2.98), different work foci (2.98), lack of organizational interest (2.77), and lack of community support (2.63).

Interestingly, lack of education and knowledge appears to be a significant factor limiting planning organizations' involvement. A majority (51 percent) of APA members cited the lack of staff trained in this area as a significant or primary explanation for their organization's limited or no involvement. No other factor received majority support (as being a significant or primary explanation) from survey respondents. In the coming years, planning practitioners, professional organizations, and academies will need to help prepare the profession by filling this gap by training planners in the area of healthy eating and community and regional food planning.

CHAPTER 4

Six Communities' Efforts
to Promote Healthy Eating

A growing number of communities are slowly transforming their food systems and food environments to promote access to affordable, nutritious, and culturally acceptable food for all people. (What is "culturally acceptable" is determined by the people of the community. Certain preferences in diet and cooking regimes can help determine what produce is most appropriate for growing and sale in a certain community.) In their struggle for food security and food justice, these communities have overcome formidable challenges, sometimes with the help of local governments and planners, and sometimes in spite of them.

In Marin County, the inclusion of food as a component of the comprehensive plan is a result of the county's visionary thinking, as well as the work of the Marin Agriculture Land Trust (MALT) and the Marin Food Policy Council (MFPC).

The six communities highlighted in this PAS Report share a common goal: the desire to improve the food system and food environment within their community. Each pursues its goal using a different strategy. We hope that the six case studies inform and inspire planners from all areas of planning about their critical role in facilitating healthy eating within their communities. The case studies were selected to represent a variety of geographic regions as well as a variety of local governments; they include Philadelphia, Pennsylvania; Madison, Wisconsin; Buffalo, New York; Portland, Oregon; Marin County, California; and Louisville, Kentucky.

The Marin County case study reports the successful inclusion of "food" as an element of a countywide comprehensive plan. The case study of Madison describes the efforts of a local government to build and strengthen its local food system in a holistic manner through programmatic, policy, and planning efforts. The Philadelphia case study describes the use of an innovative economic development strategy to bring food retail back into underserved neighborhoods. That of Louisville describes an unusual alliance—between a public housing authority and local nonprofits—in promoting healthy eating in underserved urban neighborhoods. The Portland case study describes how the institutional mechanism of a food policy council (FPC) facilitates local food policy in Portland-Multnomah metropolitan region. The Buffalo case study highlights the importance of and strategies for involving urban youth in transforming local food systems in distressed inner-city neighborhoods.

MARIN COUNTY, CALIFORNIA: COMPREHENSIVE PLANNING TO FACILITATE PRODUCTION OF HEALTHFUL FOODS AND FOOD SECURITY

When Marin County set out to update its countywide comprehensive plan in 1998, one of its key goals was to build healthy and sustainable communities. The county was determined to pay particular attention to strategies that would preserve the county's agricultural heritage as well as to ensure people's access to healthful foods. As a result, the updated comprehensive plan, adopted by the Board of Supervisors on November 6, 2007, devotes an entire section to agriculture and food, making it one of two counties (the other is Dane County, Wisconsin) in the nation to include "food" as a specific concern in a comprehensive plan. By including food security in the comprehensive plan, Marin County provides a regulatory framework for creating policies and strategies that will ensure people's access to healthful foods in the future. In Marin County, the inclusion of food as a component of the comprehensive plan is a result of the county's visionary thinking, as well as the work of the Marin Agriculture Land Trust (MALT) and the Marin Food Policy Council (MFPC). This case study offers an important example of how strategic collaboration with community partners and good timing can facilitate the inclusion of food security in a comprehensive planning process. It also describes the manner in which Marin County has incorporated food in its comprehensive plan, providing a potential model for other counties across the country.

The Threat to Marin County's Agricultural Lands and Agricultural Sector

Located in Northern California and adjacent to the ever-expanding San Francisco Bay metropolitan area, Marin County is home to 250,000 people. The county is a mix of affluent suburbs and pristine agricultural land. Of the county's 606 square miles of land, roughly 43.5 percent (169,000 acres) is devoted to agriculture. Of this land, 10 percent is public agriculture land contained in the Golden Gate National Recreation Area and Point Reyes National Seashore (www.malt.org/). Nearly one-fourth of all agricultural land in Marin County is permanently protected from subdivision and land development (Marin Countywide Plan 2007).

With a rich agricultural heritage in Marin County dating back to dairy ranch settlements of the 1800s, agriculture remains important to the local economy. Agriculture employs 1,400 people in the county on 200 farms and ranches, generating $53 million in annual gross revenues (www.malt.org). Traditionally, dairy and livestock ranches dominated Marin County's agricultural sector. According to the county's comprehensive plan, however, "many local operations have begun diversifying to increase their viability, producing row crops and value-added products such as cheese, butter, organic foods, and grass-fed beef" (Marin Countywide Plan 2007, p. 2-4).

Recently, field and orchard crops too are on the upswing as the demand for local fruits and vegetables increases. The county also supports environmentally friendly production practices and supports organic growing practices. For example, the Marin County Agricultural Commissioner's office established the first local government organic certification agency in the U.S.; it is also the first local government in California to establish a certification process for grass-fed livestock. It is therefore not surprising that from 1990 to 2002, the amount of land dedicated to organic farming in Marin County jumped from 67 acres to 1,560 acres (Marin Countywide Plan 2007).

Nonetheless, the county's prime agricultural lands, especially the working ranches, are threatened by development. Recognizing this threat, in 1980 a group of citizens formed MALT, the first land trust in the United States to focus on the preservation of agricultural land by "acquiring agricultural conservation easements on farmland in voluntary transactions" (www.malt. org). Thanks to MALT's leadership, nearly one-fourth (38,000 acres) of the agricultural lands in Marin County are permanently protected from development.

Figure 4-1. Marin County organic farmland: rolling pastures of Allstar Organics Farm, Nicasio, California.

Figure 4-2. Cows grazing at the 660-acre Straus family farm on the shores of Tomales Bay in Marin County, California.

Despite MALT's efforts, Marin County's proximity to San Francisco leaves the county vulnerable to encroaching residential development. As the price of land increases, farmers are enticed to sell their land, and the prospect for intergenerational transfers of agricultural land is diminished. Furthermore, the area struggles to attract the younger generation to the difficult work and low profit margins of farming.

Including a Specific Reference to Food in the Comprehensive Plan

Planners have struggled to protect farmland for decades. Yet, they have largely overlooked the importance of strengthening the links between producers and consumers of food in a community as a way to strengthen the local farming sector. The Marin county plan is set to change this. The plan notes that the County will:

> [P]rotect agricultural lands and work to maintain our agricultural heritage, [and] will support the production and marketing of healthy, fresh, locally grown food. (Marin Countywide Plan 2007, 1-5)

To meet this goal, the Agriculture and Food section in the Natural Systems and Agriculture Element of the plan identifies three specific goals:

1. Preservation of Agricultural Lands and Resources

2. Improved Agricultural Viability

3. Addressing Community Food Security

The first two goals are familiar to planners, but the third goal, addressing community food security, treads previously uncharted territory. By focusing on both food production as well as community food security, the plan intends to facilitate the future health of Marin County's farm economy as well as the health of its residents. We briefly describe these goals here:

Preservation of Agricultural Lands and Resources (Goal AG-1, Marin Countywide Plan 2007). To achieve this goal, the plan lists several policies, including limiting residential use of land; maintaining agricultural zoning to restrict development; and making use of sustainable water supplies to allow agriculture to thrive. The plan outlines 19 implementation strategies to enact these policies. These include, among others, revising agricultural districts to allow only agricultural activities and necessary housing, upholding the right-to-farm ordinance that protects farmers from nuisance complaints from

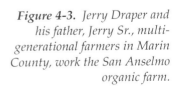

Figure 4-3. Jerry Draper and his father, Jerry Sr., multi-generational farmers in Marin County, work the San Anselmo organic farm.

Ken Smith; Ken Smith Photography

encroaching residential development, and encouraging agricultural leasing that will provide incentives to nonfarming landowners to lease their land for agricultural purposes.

Improved Agricultural Viability (Goal AG-2, Marin Countywide Plan 2007). This goal focuses on improving the economic and social viability of the agricultural industry in Marin County. This goal, and its supporting policies and strategies, are somewhat unusual in that they provide clear support for a community-based food production system, as demonstrated in selected policies listed below:

Promote Organic Certification (AG-2.1)
Support Marin Organic Certified Agriculture (MOCA) to perform local organic farm certification to comply with National Organic Program (NOP) standards.

Support Local, Organic and Grass-Fed Agriculture (AG-2.2)
Encourage and protect local, organic, grass-fed, and other ecologically sound agricultural practices, such as dry farming, including field crops and animal agriculture, as a means to increase on-farm income, diversify Marin agriculture, and provide healthy food for the local supply.

Support Small-Scale Diversification (AG-2.3)
Diversify agricultural uses and products to complement existing traditional uses, ensure the continued economic viability of the county agricultural industry, and provide increased food security.

Encourage Agricultural Processing (AG-2.4)
Encourage processing and distribution of locally produced foods to support local food security and strengthen Marin's agricultural industry.

Market Local Products (AG-2.5)
Support the efforts of local farmers and ranchers to develop more diverse and profitable markets related to agriculture, including a permanent public market and direct marketing to local and regional restaurants for Marin County agricultural products.

Support Small-Scale Crop Production (AG-2.6)
Encourage small-scale row crop production that contributes to local food security on appropriate sites throughout the county.

Preserve and Promote Mariculture [Mariculture is a type of acquaculture involving the production of organisms (plants and animals) for food in open oceans and seas, or in confined areas of marine bodies that are filled with sea-water.] (AG-2.7)
Support maricultural usage of tidelands and onshore production areas.

Increase Knowledge of Agriculture (AG-2.10)
Raise the level of public awareness and understanding of Marin County agriculture, including its ecological, economic, open space, and cultural value, and its importance to local food security.

Facilitate the Intergenerational Transfer of Agricultural Land (AG-2.11)
Encourage and support transfer through inheritance, sale, or lease of agricultural properties to future generations of ranchers and farmers.

Figure 4-4. David Little (in back) and employee Cleto Gurrola harvest potatoes by hand at Little Organic farm.

To achieve these policy objectives, the plan outlines the following implementation programs that offers a model for how other local governments can support local food production systems:

Provide adequate staffing to respond to expected annual growth for all Marin producers and handlers that wish to obtain organic certification. Develop incentives to encourage farmers and ranchers to transition from conventional farming practices to organic, grass-fed, or other ecologically sound techniques such as dry farming, or "beyond organic" (addressing ethical criteria not included in USDA organic standards). (AG-2.a)

Review and amend the Development Code as appropriate to include new and/or modified criteria and standards for agricultural processing and sales while limiting uses that are not compatible with sustainable agriculture. ...Continue to [ensure] that the new criteria and standards are consistent with the County's goals of improved agricultural viability and preservation and restoration of the natural environment. (AG-2.c)

Allow agricultural producers to use small, tasteful, on-site signage to advertise their products and services, and consider the establishment of a community based program of discreet, off-site signs for directing the public to on-farm sales areas. (AG-2.f)

Amend the Development Code to include mariculture as a conditional use in the C-RSP or other zoning districts as appropriate for lands located along the shoreline of Tomales Bay. (AG-2.g)

Promote the distribution of local foods through the Community Food Bank. Continue to offer farmers' market food coupons to food stamp and WIC recipients but increase the individual allotment. (AG-2.j)

Support sustainable agriculture education, such as the Food for Thought curricula, in local schools, including the College of Marin. (AG-2.k)

Promote public appreciation of agriculture by supporting organizations and agencies that carry out educational programs. (AG-2.l)

Identify agricultural areas with placement of appropriate directional signs in an effort to inform residents and visitors of the importance of agriculture in Marin. (AG-2.m)

Assess the effects of local, State, and federal policies on agriculture, and determine future policy directions. (AG-2.n)

Figure 4-5. Serge Tolentin loads the olive harvest at the McEvoy Ranch in Marin County, which contains 18,000 olive trees spread over 80 acres.

Address Community Food Security (Goal AG-3, Marin Countywide Plan 2007). The third goal within the Agriculture and Food section of Marin's Countywide Plan focuses on promoting community food security for residents. The plan defines the goal of community food security as follows:

> Increase the diversity of locally produced foods to give residents greater access to a healthy, nutritionally adequate diet. (Marin County Comprehensive Plan, 2007)

The Community plan identifies three broad policies, along with implementation strategies, to achieve this goal:

> Support local food production (AG 3.1)
>
> Promote local and organic food (AG 3.2)
>
> Enhance food security education (AG 3.3)

To implement these policies, the following implementation strategies are outlined:

Encourage community gardens (AG 3.a) Allow community gardens on underutilized land or where such use would complement current use, and amend the Development Code to require space for on-site community gardens in new residential developments of 10 units or greater. Work with community-based organizations to manage such gardens using ecologically sound techniques and to provide on-site water if available.

Provide Community Education (AG3.b) Provide community education regarding organic and other ecologically sound techniques of farming and the benefits of its produce. Raise awareness of farmers' market dates and times.

Promote Edible Landscaping (AG-3.c) Encourage fruit trees or other edible landscaping when possible in new development and when renewing planting on County property where appropriate. Include the replacement of irrigated ornamentals with drought-resistant edible plants, as appropriate.

Use Locally Grown and/or Organic Foods in County Services (AG-3.d) Develop and adopt a food policy and procurement program that incorporates organic and locally grown foods into cafeteria services, the jail, and County-sponsored events.

Promote Organic Food in Schools. (AG-3.e) Support school programs, including on-site gardens, that incorporate organic foods into school meals.

Support Local Groups. (AG-3.f) Support the efforts of local groups such as the MFPC that make recommendations and support forums addressing sustainable food systems.

The Agriculture and Food section of the plan, like all other sections, concludes with a detailed action plan which identifies the priority level of each policy/strategy, the time line for achieving it, benchmarks for evaluating progress, as well as the agency responsible for implementation (see Figure 4-6). For example, the plan calls for an additional 37,500 acres of agricultural lands to be preserved using agricultural easements, and an increase of annual farmers' market sales 15 percent by 2015.

The Agriculture and Food section of the plan, like all other sections, concludes with a detailed action plan which identifies the priority level of each policy/strategy, the time line for achieving it, benchmarks for evaluating progress, as well as the agency responsible for implementation.

Figure 4-6. Benchmarks for food-related recommendations in the Marin Countywide Plan.

MARIN COUNTYWIDE PLAN

Programs	Responsibility	Potential Funding	Priority	Time Frame
AG-2.n – Support Food and Agriculture Assessment Panel.	Agricultural Commissioner, UCCE-FA	Will require additional grants or revenue[3]	Medium	Med. Term
AG-3.a – Encourage Community Gardens.	CDA, Agricultural Commissioner, UCCE-FA, DPW, MCOSD	Existing budget	Low	Ongoing
AG-3.b – Provide Community Education.	UCCE-FA, Agricultural Commissioner, CBO's	Existing budget and may require additional grants or revenue[3]	Medium	Ongoing
AG-3.c – Promote Edible Landscaping.	CDA, Agricultural Commissioner, UCCE-FA, MCOSD	Existing budget	Low	Ongoing
AG-3.d – Use Locally Grown and/or Organic Foods in County Services.	Cultural Services, Agricultural Commissioner, UCCE-FA	Existing budget and may require additional grants or revenues, as well as Incentive Payments to Growers	High	Ongoing
AG-3.e – Promote Organic Food in Schools.	UCCE-FA, Agricultural Commissioner, Marin Food Policy Council, CBO's	Existing budget and may require additional grants or revenue[3]	Medium	Ongoing
AG-3.f – Support Local Groups.	Agricultural Commissioner, CBO's, UCCE-FA	Existing budget and may require additional grants or revenue[3]	Medium	Ongoing

Marin County, California

How Did Food Issues Get to the Planning Commission's Table?

The synergistic focus on food production and healthy eating within Marin's Comprehensive plan is anything but a matter of chance. It is the result of a well-designed comprehensive planning process and an effective working relationship between the MFPC and the Marin County Plan Commission. According to Alex Hinds, Marin County Planning Director, the county, as part of the planning process, created working groups to lead the revision process of the comprehensive plan. Hinds appointed people who had cutting-edge ideas that would foster creative solutions and would limit political fighting between interest groups. The Natural Systems Element working group, which drafted the Agriculture and Food section for the Comprehensive Plan, included both farmers and members of the FPC.

The FPC, for its part, was an organized and active participant in the planning process. Following the county's announcement of its intention to update its countywide plan in 1998, the volunteer-led FPC voted to devote its time and resources to actively participate in the planning process by developing food-related recommendations for the plan and submitting them for consideration during the plan revision process. (This process was greatly facilitated by the fact that a member of the FPC simultaneously served as a member of the County Planning Commission.) The FPC was well-positioned to take on this task: it had previously undertaken significant research and analysis on local food security issues, and had a standing policy document on local food security reflecting the larger community's sentiments on sustainable agriculture and community food security. Using this information as a starting point, the FPC drafted food-related recommendations and submitted them to the Natural Systems Element working group, structuring and organizing the recommendations in a way that would easily make their way into subsequent plan revisions. Facilitated by the planning staff, the working group deliberated on and finalized the text provided by the FPC to make it suitable for inclusion in the comprehensive plan. With more than 30 pages of well-researched recommendations provided by the FPC, the working group was well-equipped to draft the food section of the plan.

Lessons for Planners

The achievements in Marin County highlight the importance of civic leadership, partnerships, preparation, and good timing for incorporating food issues in the comprehensive planning process. At the time of Marin's plan revision, the completely volunteer-led FPC had an effective working partnership with the County Plan Commission, including the fortuitous fact that a member of the FPC also served on the Plan Commission. The FPC was also well-prepared to provide meaningful input to the planning process. Prior to the planning process, the FPC had successfully engaged the community through outreach and education to create a policy statement about local food security. These materials formed the basis for materials subsequently submitted by the FPC and subsequently incorporated into the comprehensive plan.

It is important to highlight the critical importance of good timing in planning for food. In Marin, the intention to update the countywide plan was announced in 1998, and the plan was finally adopted in 2007. MFPC members recognized the strategic importance of timing their efforts with the countywide planning process. The FPC took approximately two years to draft the language for the countywide plan and submitted it to the county early enough to allow for a thorough review, discussion, and eventual incorporation (with some modifications) in the countywide plan.

Nonetheless, the inclusion of food security was not entirely an easy process in Marin County. Marin County Planning Director, Alex Hinds, notes that although people are not generally opposed to the idea of food security, less support exists for regulations that affect agriculture and land use. For example, during the public comment period in the planning process, citizens were considerably opposed to limiting the size of houses on agricultural land. Thus, many rewrites were undertaken to ensure that the plan was acceptable to all stakeholders.

Hinds advises planners and planning departments interested in incorporating food security into comprehensive plan to spend considerable energy on education and outreach:

> Start with the education and outreach policies and activities. Get people to recognize agriculture's importance to the culture and heritage of a place. Encourage farmers to host festivals, visits to the farm, and hay rides. Show people the importance of growing local food. Then when the time is right and the regulations are needed, introduce the regulations that are necessary to maintaining agricultural land. If timed right and supported by the right people, land use regulations [face less] opposition. (Hinds 2007)

Marin County moves forward with a strong comprehensive plan in place that addresses food security today and for future generations. Healthy eating and food security cannot be addressed without addressing the related problem of agricultural preservation. The county's efforts, with the collaboration of local organizations, FPCs, and local citizens, show that comprehensive plans can be used to achieve both of these goals.

MADISON, WISCONSIN: INCREASING ACCESS TO HEALTHFUL FOODS BY STRENGTHENING THE LOCAL FOOD SYSTEM

Every Saturday, 300 vendors set up at the Dane County Farmers' Market in Madison to sell fresh fruits, vegetables, baked goods, and other locally made products , including honey, syrup, and cheeses. University students gather to chat or play Frisbee on the grassy area of Capitol Square, which hosts the

Planning Director, Alex Hinds, notes that although people are not generally opposed to the idea of food security, less support exists for regulations that affect agriculture and land use.

Although the public transit system is extensive and relatively convenient in Madison, it is still difficult to rely on bus transportation for grocery shopping due to the potential need for to transfer routes, carry heavy bags, and keep frozen or refrigerated items cold.

farmers' market. Standing at the farmers' market, it is hard to imagine that access to healthy food is or ever was a concern in the capital of the Dairy State. In Madison and surrounding Dane County, people's connection to food and agriculture remains strong. The county is one of the most agriculturally productive in the state. A Community Supported Agriculture Farm, Troy Gardens, is located within city limits. Thirty city-funded community garden sites, totaling 1,600 garden plots, including one of the largest gardens in the country, Eagle Heights, exist on the University of Wisconsin campus. For the most part, the city is free from large-scale "food deserts" or neighbordhoods that have no access to stores that sell healthful foods.

But Madison's healthful food environment did not happen overnight nor came about by chance. A series of complementary programmatic, policy, and regulatory actions by a partnership of city and county governments and community groups in the region have facilitated the creation of a food environment that offers healthy eating options to residents. This case study illustrates the use of a web of interconnected efforts to create a long-term healthy eating environment.

Threatened Farmland and Inadequate Grocery Stores

Madison is located in south central Wisconsin. The state capital and home to the state university, in 2006, the city's population was approximately 214,000 people. Madison covers only 85 square miles of Dane County's roughly 1,200 square miles. Although small in land area, the city comprises almost half of the county's population of nearly 464,000. Eighty-nine percent of Madison residents are white, 4 percent are African American, 3.5 percent are Asian, and 3.5 percent fall under the "other" racial category.

According to Mark Olinger, the director of the city's Department of Planning and Economic and Community Development, Madison does not suffer from extreme food deserts, as do other communities. According to Olinger, the city has experienced the problem of large grocery stores leaving the city for suburban locations. Five large grocery stores closed in the period of 2003-2004, and all were close to census block groups with large numbers of households without vehicles. Olinger also expresses concern about losing farmland in Dane County due to the combination of development pressures and decreasing interest in farming in younger generations.

A planning exercise conducted by graduate students at the University of Wisconsin-Madison in 1997 foretold the planning director's concerns. *Fertile Ground: Planning for the Madison/Dane County Food System* cited a growing population and development pressures as the primary threat to food access: "In fact, growth in the form of urban, suburban and exurban sprawl, may be the single largest barrier to a food secure future in Dane County" (Allan et al. 1997). At that time, Dane County was losing farmland at the second highest rate of all counties in the nation.

Echoing Olinger's sentiments, Majid Allan, a planner with the Dane County Planning Department emphasizes access to healthy food as an ongoing challenge for Madison residents. The closing of grocery stores in low-income neighborhoods makes shopping for fresh foods difficult since longer trip distances lead to fewer trips; residents stock up on items that will keep longer to reduce their trips to the grocery store. Although the public transit system is extensive and relatively convenient in Madison, it is still difficult to rely on bus transportation for grocery shopping due to the potential need for to transfer routes, carry heavy bags, and keep frozen or refrigerated items cold.

Jerome Kaufman, FAICP, a retired professor of urban planning from the University at Wisconsin who has long been involved in Madison's food policy network, dissects the problem from the perspective of supply and demand. On the supply side, the majority of farmers in Dane County are dairy farmers. The few farmers that grow produce struggle to compete with the corporate food industry in the local market. Additionally, there is no central processing and distribution center that connects rural farmers to urban markets, such as grocery stores and restaurants. Officials from the city and county cite the lack of effective distribution mechanism as an ongoing barrier to healthy eating in the region. On the demand side, Madison is likely doing better than most communities, with a highly educated and relatively food aware population (Stevens and Raja 2001). However education and outreach is still needed to communicate the importance of healthy eating to the average resident.

Comprehensive Efforts to Promote Healthy Eating and Food Security

The Madison region showcases a variety of programs, supported by the city and county, to address healthy eating. These programs are frequently operated by nonprofits and supported by local governments.

The Dane County Farmers' Market: A healthy food destination for the region. Farmers' markets have long been a part of the Madison's urban fabric. The first organized farmers' market in the city, The Dane County Farmers' Market, was founded in 1972 and now operates on the capitol square—the public area surrounding the capitol building. The country's largest producer-only farmers' market, the Dane County Farmers' Market has about 300 vendors and operates from May until November on Wednesdays, and year round on Saturdays. The market's vibrant atmosphere, especially on Saturdays, attracts local art vendors and musicians who are allowed to set up stalls along the periphery of the market. The market is not only a place to buy and support local agriculture, but has become a significant community destination to meet friends, interact, and spend time.

The Dane County Farmers' Market is by far the largest and best-known market in the region, but numerous other markets exist throughout the city and county. The Department of Planning and Community and Economic Development has been actively engaged in ensuring the success of farmers' markets in Madison. One such effort included working with farmers affected by the renovation of the street off the capitol square where the Wednesday Market was held to ensure that the new space would be functional for the farmers. A second project with another nascent Madison farmers' market involved Community Development Authority staff working with market supporters to obtain a lease for the planned farmers market. Additional support from the city included the provision of electricity to the parking lot to power coolers for produce, the renewal of the site license for the market for a second year, and assistance in securing the variance request for a signage permit for the market.

The city also changed its zoning regulations to better accommodate farmers' markets. Previously, farmers' markets were not permitted in some zones that would seem appropriate for them (office zones, for example). The city is also in the process of creating the institutional and physical infrastructure to support the creation of a year round permanent farmers' market by the year 2010.

The Troy Gardens development: Healthful food and affordable housing in the city. Troy Gardens is a 31-acre site, held in a land trust, on Madison's north side that includes community gardens, an organic CSA farm, and an affordable housing development. The history of the Troy Gardens development highlights the power of people in transforming traditional planning processes. Area residents had been gardening on four acres of vacant land near the grounds of the Mendota Mental Health Institute, a state-run mental health facility, since 1980. In 1995, the State of Wisconsin decided to put the

Farmers' markets have long been a part of the Madison's urban fabric. The first organized farmers' market in the city, The Dane County Farmers' Market, was founded in 1972 and now operates on the capitol square—the public area surrounding the capitol building.

four acres, and an additional 15 acres that lay adjacent to the four, on a surplus land list with the intention of selling it. In 1996, an additional 16-acre undeveloped site was added to the surplus list. Under threat of losing their community garden, dog-walking area, and nature sanctuary, local residents organized against the sale. The concerned residents and gardeners, assisted by a variety of organizations and groups, including the Northside Planning Council, the Madison Area Community Land Trust (MACLT), the Urban Open Space Foundation, the Community Action Coalition Garden Program, and the University of Wisconsin-Madison, eventually formed the Troy Gardens Coalition.

The coalition approached the threat of losing the land as an opportunity to shape the neighborhood's future. The group created an innovative land-use plan for the site that called for a mix of housing and agricultural use. In 1997, the state agreed to take the entire 31-acre site off the surplus land list and granted the coalition a 16-year lease to use the land for community gardens and open space. In 1998, the City of Madison accepted the coalition's concept plan for the area, and Troy Gardens was born. In 1998, the state agreed to extend the lease to 50 years with the option to buy the property in the future. After three long years of fundraising, MACLT, with support from the City of Madison, purchased the property in December of 2001 (www.troygardens.org).

Unique planning features and a mix of innovative land tenure arrangements make Troy Gardens a model project for affordable housing and healthy living. The ownership of the 31-acre site is held in a land trust by MACLT on behalf of the Northside community. Twenty-six acres of the land are leased to the Friends of Troy Gardens. This land, which is also held under a conservation easement by Urban Open Space Foundation (UOSF), a local nonprofit organization, includes a five-acre CSA farm, community gardens, prairie restoration areas, and natural trails. The remaining five acres are dedicated for affordable housing units developed by the MACLT.

Figure 4-7. Troy Gardens concept plan.This unique development includes 30 affordable (co)housing units, a five-acre urban community supported agriculture farm, and community gardens on a 31-acre site held in a land trust.

Friends of Troy Gardens

On the 26 acres of land leased to them, the Friends of Troy Gardens promote land stewardship using inclusive, community-based decision making to meet the following goals:

- Use the land sustainably
- Increase food security for Madison's Northside residents
- Develop ecological and food literacy programs
- Engage various stakeholders in creating a thriving community around the land
- Create attractive public green space
- Become an economically stable and financially sustainable organization

A more recent venture of the group focuses more directly on promoting healthy eating. The Healthful Foods, Healthy Communities Project (HFHC), a joint venture of numerous food advocacy groups, including the Research, Education, Action, and Policy on Food Group (REAP), the Friends of Troy Gardens, the Madison Area Community Supported Agriculture Coalition, and

Figure 4-8. The residents of these affordable, compact, mixed-income, residential units in Troy Gardens have plots in the adjacent community garden.

Jessica Kozlowski Russell

the University of Wisconsin-Extension Nutrition Education Program, focuses on providing education about and access to healthful foods to young people in three different "life spaces"—schools, homes, and neighborhoods through a variety of activities. These activities include: education programs on gardening, agriculture, nutrition, and food preparation; provision of community meals; and reduced costs for locally grown food. The project intends to achieve the following outcomes:

- Increase the consumption of high quality, nutritious fruits and vegetables among Madison's Northside community
- Build skills in food production and preparation
- Improve understanding and knowledge about healthy food choices

On the remaining five acres, MACLT in collaboration with the city's Department of Planning and Economic and Community Development, has built 30 affordable housing units using green technologies. According to MACLT:

> Housing units built on Troy Gardens are sold at a lower than market value because buyers do not have to pay for the land, which is owned by the Madison Area Community Land Trust. Twenty of the 30 planned homes have been sold as land trust homes to first-time homebuyers at or below 80 percent of the median income level for Dane County. These were priced under market value with a restriction on how much profit can be made when units are resold, so that will be permanently affordable to future buyers. The remaining ten units were sold on the open market as conventional homes. Units range from 2-4 bedrooms with a variety of floor plans. All units are fully handicapped accessible on the first floor.

Thanks to effective community organizing and a progressive planning model, residents of the Troy Gardens development have access to affordable housing as well as healthful foods.

Community Gardens: Supporting Urban Agriculture to Produce Healthy Food

Troy Gardens is not the only development that has access to healthful food in the city of Madison. About 30 community gardens are scattered throughout the city. The gardens vary in size; the largest of the gardens, Eagle Heights, encompasses 400 plots, making it one of the largest community gardens in the nation. These 30 gardens cover 13 acres of land and support 1,600 individual garden plots (Madison Comprehensive Plan).

In Madison, community gardens are supported directly by city funds. Madison is one of the few communities in the country that funds community gardens through its Community Development Block Grants (CDBG) program. The CDBG commission, which is responsible for developing priority areas for the funds, sees community gardens as a tool for build a sense of community. The Department of Planning and Community and Economic Development provides funding to the Community Action Coalition, a local nonprofit group, of about $25,000-30,000 per year to hire a community gardens manager. As noted below, community gardens are also recognized in the city's comprehensive plan.

Figure 4-9. Community gardens at Troy Garden in Madison, Wisconsin.

Despite the city's support, gardens often face land tenure threats and are often viewed as temporary uses of land. According to Olinger, as a result of this challenge in ownership status, several community gardens have been lost. The different land-use policies of governments are also a challenge, as the state and the city sometimes have different goals when it comes to public land dispensation. In a current example, the city is in negotiation with the state regarding the redevelopment of a parcel of state-owned land in the city. The parcel is the site of a one-acre community garden, and the redevelopment has forced relocation of the garden space, which was ongoing at the time of the preparation of this PAS Report. As a general goal, the city aims to create one community garden for every 2,000 households and plans to extend garden leases on city-owned land to five years.

Facilitating Grocery Store Development

Madison has an interest in maintaining grocery stores in the city and ensuring food access to all residents. The city promotes and uses creative solutions to provide residents with access to quality food and healthy eating opportunities. It not only actively seeks grocers and food retailers, but it provides financial assistance and/or city-space or city-owned facilities to encourage them to locate in areas that might be otherwise underserved.

In one case, an independent neighborhood grocery store closed. The site sat vacant for three years as the city debated how the site how it should be redeveloped. The neighborhood and the mayor wanted a grocery store there, though the developers had targeted the site for condominiums. The city did not want the site to be redeveloped for condominiums because it would mean the loss of the grocer. As a result, the local Community Development Authority adopted Redevelopment District Legislation to avoid undesirable uses moving onto the site and offered assistance to investors willing to develop a grocery store on site. The solution was found in a mixed-use development that included a grocery store and condominiums, as well as underground parking for the store. Financial assistance through tax incremental financing (TIF) revenues in the amount of $2.5 million helped underwrite the costs of underground parking for the grocery store. The specialty grocer, Trader Joe's, moved into the new space in 2006.

Madison has used other smaller grants on projects through the planning department as well. One went to a major food retail cooperative store (the Willy Street Co-op) to assist them with relocation to a new and larger location. The city's urban design commission, the planning commission, and their staff also work with architects, vendors, and farmers to provide guidance on site selection and design of food retail spaces.

Policy Initiatives: Developing a Food Policy Council

In 2005, a countywide FPC was established by the Dane County board at the recommendation of the Local Food Policy Advisory Subcommittee, a citizen advisory group appointed in 2004 by Supervisor Kyle Richmond, the Chair of Dane County's Environment, Agriculture, and Natural Resources Committee, to study the issues affecting local food systems. The Dane County Food Policy Council is a collaborative effort between public and private groups. In its first year of creation, the City of Madison, Dane County, and the University of Madison-Wisconsin contributed $5,000 each to establish an FPC (Dillon and Harris 2007). Staff from the Dane County Planning Department and University of Wisconsin Extension provided support to the Food Council in its second year.

An advisory body to the government, the council is comprised of 12 citizen members, each of whom serves two terms. The 12 members represent many interest groups, including small- and large-scale farmers, hunger advocates, nonprofit organizations, university professors, farmers' market managers, and urban planners. The council functions through several subcommittees that take on focused tasks. The council's most recent focus has been on:

- increasing the vitality of farmers' markets and making them more accessible to vulnerable populations (e.g., through the use of WIC vouchers, and Electronic Benefits Transfer);

- promoting purchase of local fresh food by county-run institutions; a recent county resolution facilitated by the council encourages the use of locally purchased foods in the county jail, juvenile detention center, and senior centers;

- increasing access to fresh fruits and vegetables for low-income households through the expansion of a market basket program that provides baskets at a cost ranging from $8-$26 per week (Dillon and Harris 2007); and

- outreach and education within the community on a variety of healthy eating and food issues.

Figure 4-10. Children with harvest from children's garden at Troy Garden in Madison, Wisconsin.

Friends of Troy Gardens

Incorporating Food into the Mayor's Healthy Cities Initiative

Healthy eating and food issues also receive support from the executive branches of local government in the Madison region. Dave Cieslewicz, Madison's mayor, encouraged the development of a healthy economy in which food would be a considered an element through his 2004 Healthy Cities Initiative. The initiative incorporated the issue of healthful food access through two elements: a food production facility (Central Agricultural Food Facility), and a year-round farmers' market.

The Central Agricultural Food Facility is a proposed processing facility that would allow the creation of value-added products from a variety of locally grown foods. Direct effects would include food for local consumption, broader markets for food-businesses, and food-related jobs and job training for residents. The year-round farmers' market or public market has been under discussion for a long time among the Department of Planning and Community and Economic Development, the Madison Community Foundation, and other local foundations. The Department of Planning and Community and Economic Development awarded $100,000 to study the feasibility and potential location of a public market in the city. The public market project is now being actively pursued, and a preliminary site for the market has been identified. The plan is to break ground in 2009 and open the public market in 2010.

In addition to the Healthy Cities Initiative, the mayor's office developed a report, *Grocery Stores in City Neighborhoods*, which documents the important role the city should play in supporting food retailers in order to ensure equitable access to food (Stouder 2004). The report is a springboard for directing food retail development in underserved areas.

Setting a Course for the Future: Inclusion of Food in Comprehensive Plans

The planning departments in Madison and Dane County are using the traditional tool of comprehensive planning to facilitate healthy eating and food security issues. Inclusion of these issues in comprehensive plans provides a basis for policy and regulatory reform to improve the region's food environment.

The city's 2006 comprehensive plan addresses the food system in its Agriculture and Natural Resources element. The plan acknowledges that while the city is "essentially an urban place," it has a role to play in "protecting and supporting local agricultural activities and in the preservation of the county's farmland." The plan notes that, while the 597 acres of agricultural land available in the city in 2004 would eventually be developed, some "agricultural uses will be permanent features of the city's urban fabric" (City of Madison Comprehensive Plan 2006, Volume II, 6-5). In particular, the following features are noted:

- Troy Gardens, a Community Supported Agriculture farm

- Thirteen acres of community gardens, comprising 1600 individual plots

- Farmers' markets in the city that sell produce from the Madison area and from the larger region

- A food preparation center serving several local restaurants and institutions

Figure 4-11. Permanently protected community-supported agriculture farm at Troy Garden.

Given widespread community support for the above goals, the plan outlines two key goals pertaining to the city's food system in the Agricultural Resources subsection (City of Madison Comprehensive Plan, Volume II, 6-16):

1. Maintain the region's status as one of the nation's most productive and economically viable food production areas; and

2. Maintain existing agricultural operations in the City and encourage new, smaller farming operations such as Community Supported Agricultural Farms.

To achieve these goals, the plan outlines four objectives and related policies:

1. Encourage the preservation of farming operations within the City where it is economically feasible and compatible with surrounding land uses (Objective 11, Volume II, 6-16).

   - Identify, map, and maintain a database of agricultural operations in the City.

   - Coordinate with the County to educate farmers with operations in the City about incentive programs that will help them continue farming or to sell their land to farmers with interest in smaller-scale agricultural operations such as farmette development and Community Supported Agricultural Farming.

2. Identify areas on the City's periphery suitable for long-term preservation for diverse agricultural enterprises and community separation (Objective 12, Volume II, 6-17).

   • Cooperate with adjoining towns and villages and Dane County to protect identified long-term preservation areas for the benefit and use of current and future generations.

   • Encourage unique agricultural uses, such as apiaries, orchards, vineyards, and other agricultural land uses, that are compatible with urban uses.

3. Promote the sale of foods grown in Dane County (Objective 13, Volume II, 6-17).

   • Support Dane County's efforts to promote and develop direct-marketing alternatives for agricultural foods and products.

   • Support Dane County's efforts to educate the general public on the value that agriculture production and business add to the Dane County economy.

   • Support Dane County's efforts to help entrepreneurs plan, start, and grow new enterprises that capture value from agriculture.

   • Support Dane County's efforts to establish a Food Council to coordinate issues and policies related to locally grown foods.

4. Protect existing community gardens in the City and establish additional areas for new community gardens (Objective 14, Volume II, 6-18).

   • Expand community gardening opportunities in the City; consider using City surplus property and parkland to do this.

   • Strive to create one community garden for every 2,000 households in the City.

   • Design aesthetically pleasing community gardens appropriate to the neighborhoods where they are located.

   • Extend leases of community gardens on City-owned property to five years.

   • Establish permanent community gardens on City-owned land or in City parks where possible.

The Dane County Comprehensive Plan, adopted on October 18, 2007, also reinforces the planning efforts of the city by focusing on agricultural preservation, maintaining the economic viability of agriculture, continuing educational efforts, and supporting the FPC. The county outlines a number of goals, objectives, and policies in the Agricultural, Natural, and Cultural Resources, and Economic Development sections of the plan (Chapters 5 and 6, Dane County Comprehensive Plan 2007).

The tools that the county will use to achieve these goals include traditional and nontraditional market-based and regulatory approaches for protecting farmland, such as exploring the use of purchase of development rights, and transfer of development rights to limit the conversion of agricultural land to other uses, and directing urban development away from agricultural land. In addition to paying attention to the supply side of food production (i.e., farmland preservation), the plan calls for increasing demand for local foods through aggressive and strategic marketing efforts to increase the sale of Dane County agricultural products. In addition to strengthening food production (farming) within the county, the plan reaffirms support for strengthening the overall local food system. Selected relevant goals, objectives, and policies from the plan are listed here (Dane County Comprehensive Plan 2007, Chapter 5, p. 34-37):

Goals and objectives

1. Identify areas of Dane County suitable for long-term preservation and viability of diverse agricultural enterprises and resources. Protect or encourage protection of those areas for the benefit and use of current and future generations.

   • Minimize the amount of land converted from agricultural use to accommodate permitted non-farm development.

   • Develop and implement new tools, such as Purchase of Agricultural Conservation Easements (PACE), Transfer of Development Rights (TDR), and conservation subdivisions to meet agricultural resource goals.

   • Implement fees and other financial mechanisms to support agricultural preservation efforts and create a disincentive for unnecessary conversion of agricultural land.

2. Maintain Dane County's status as one of the nation's most productive and economically viable agricultural areas. Keep farming economically viable in Dane County through the 21st century.

   • Ordinances and regulations, which restrict noise, odors, keeping of animals, or other activities that could inhibit typical farm operations, should not apply in locally designated agricultural areas.

   • Actively promote and develop direct-marketing alternatives for all agricultural foods and products.

   • Develop marketing tools to promote use of Dane County grown goods in local, regional, and wider markets.

   • Continue and strengthen efforts to educate farmers about cost-saving measures.

   • Educate the general public on the value that agricultural production/agri-business adds to the Dane County economy.

     • Help entrepreneurs plan, start, and grow new enterprises that capture value from agriculture.

     • Provide information about modern agricultural production to foster understanding and tolerance between farmers and their residential neighbors.

     • Consider whether any new county regulations would put Dane County farmers at a competitive disadvantage to farmers in adjoining counties.

Selected policies

   • Develop and implement a comprehensive economic development program to support, expand, and enhance agriculture as a viable economic activity in Dane County.

   • Make sure county-funded highway and other transportation improvements and plans take into account the needs of farmers.

   • Work to develop viable, affordable options for rural farm families needing health insurance.

   • Continue to support the Dane County Food Council to:

     • coordinate efforts to build a stronger local food system;

     • advise county government to address food system issues, particularly aimed at strengthening the capacity of the local and regional food system assist in food-related education;

     • gather relevant data and information;

     • play a coordinating role among groups in the local food system, and;

     • develop policies to address food system issues.

Figure 4-12. *Chicken coop at Troy Garden in Madison.*

How Did Food and Healthy Eating Become Planning Issues in the Madison Region?

The roots of Madison's innovative and comprehensive approach to ensuring access to healthy food go back in many ways to the University of Wisconsin-Madison. In the mid-1990s, Professors Jerome Kaufman and Kameshwari Pothukuchi of the university's Department of Urban and Regional Planning supervised one of the earliest graduate planning studios on food systems, training the first cohort of planning students in community and regional food planning. The studio, which was funded by the Madison Food System Project, an initiative of the Kellogg Foundation, resulted in a report on Dane County's Food System (*Fertile Ground*). Following up on the success of the food planning studio, the Department of Urban and Regional Planning incorporated food systems studies into its curriculum. Graduates of the program, such as Majid Allan, went on to apply their skills in community and regional food planning to their work within the city and county governments (e.g., Majid Allan and Olivia Parry, Dane County; Linda Horvath, City of Madison; Heather Stouder, City of Madison) and nonprofit organizations work (e.g., Mark Stevens, Research Action Food Policy Group). Under Kaufman's directorship, the Madison Food System Project (MFSP) also provided considerable research and staff support to other food initiatives in the region. For example, the MFSP project provided staff assistance to the Community Gardens Advisory Committee; on behalf of the committee, MFSP staff authored the city's first community gardens plan (Raja 2000). MFSP also provided staff support for the Research, Education, Action and Policy on Food Group (REAP).

Along with the knowledge generation and capacity building on food-related issues by the university, local citizen groups exhibited a strong interest in food issues. Because of this interest and activism, County Board Supervisor Kyle Richmond, the chair of the newly formed Dane County Environment, Agriculture and Natural Resources Committee, established a food policy advisory subcommittee in 2004. The members of this subcommittee conducted research on the Dane County food system and prepared and submitted recommendations to the county government. A key recommendation, which was adopted despite reservations by some County Board members, was the creation of a permanent FPC at the county level. A key ally in facilitating this process was Majid Allan, a planner with Dane County Planning Department and a graduate of the University of Wisconsin's Master's in Urban Planning program. Allan provided administrative and staff support to the food advisory group, and helped them navigate the political intricacies of functioning as a citizen advisory board.

Madison's success in promoting healthy eating and access to nutritious food cannot be credited to one organization or individual. Rather, Madison's progress is due to the interconnected web of mutually reinforcing programs, policies, and regulations, as well as a strong political and cultural support for agriculture. Allan notes that the region "has some of the most agriculturally productive land of any metropolitan area in the country, and area residents generally agree on the need to preserve that land for future generations." He adds that the area "has a strong 'pro-local' tradition on food, and with rising fuel prices, and increasing interest in sustainability, further strengthening of the local food system is a logical outgrowth of these local traditions. [A] strong agricultural tradition provides broad consensus on improving the overall food system. Whether one's concerns are largely ethical, social, or economic, most can agree that increasing local [food] production for local consumption is a win-win proposition."

Lessons for Planners

Planners can help citizen groups navigate a complex political system. For example, Majid Allan used his position as a county planner to help food advisory groups to be an effective participant in local government decision making about food issues. Like many counties with both urban and rural constituencies, the political system in Dane County sometimes makes it difficult to get programs or policies adopted. Allan worked with the advisory group to build coalitions in support of the food policy council. While Allan is quick to point out that he and his staff provided limited resources, his role in navigating the county's political system was invaluable. Acting as a liaison between citizen groups, planning organizations, and elected officials is an important function for planners.

Plans, policies, and associated regulatory reform need to be based on well-documented examinations of current conditions. Much of this research in Madison came from the University of Wisconsin and graduate students in the Department of Urban and Regional Planning. Planners can play a critical role in assisting efforts of nonprofit organizations by providing staff support and resources for conducting research, and by functioning as bridges between government and other researchers.

Finally, planners have a role and responsibility to educate themselves and their professional colleagues about food systems and related public health issues. Working in cross-disciplinary environments and considering both near-term and long-term repercussions of planning and action are the hallmarks of the planning profession and certainly necessary for building healthy food environments.

Madison exemplifies a diversified and increasingly integrated approach to facilitate healthy eating through a mix of programs, policies, and plans. There are old and new programs for food access and healthy eating, including an established and growing network of farmers' markets and the Troy Garden urban farm. Madison's innovative planning approach values the connection between the rural and urban landscape and the impact of this connection on

Planners can help citizen groups navigate a complex political system. For example, Majid Allan used his position as a county planner to help food advisory groups to be an effective participant in local government decision making about food issues.

the daily lives of Madison's residents. Planners can use Madison and Dane County as an example for understanding how programmatic, policy, and regulatory initiatives work together to reinforce healthy eating objectives.

PHILADELPHIA: BRINGING FOOD RETAIL TO UNDERSERVED NEIGHBORHOODS THROUGH INNOVATIVE FINANCING

Progress Plaza, the nation's oldest African-American-owned shopping center, is reopening with a new 46,000-square-foot Fresh Grocer taking center stage as the plaza's anchor store. Located in North Philadelphia, the plaza had fallen victim to disinvestment and disrepair since the previous supermarket left in 1998. The redeveloped plaza will bring fresh, nutritious food and vitality back to the neighborhood. This redevelopment project is being made possible in part by an innovative financing strategy, the Fresh Food Financing Initiative, which was created in 2004 through a partnership between The Food Trust, The Reinvestment Fund, The Greater Philadelphia Urban Affairs Coalition, and the State of Pennsylvania.

The Lack of Supermarkets in Philadelphia's Low-Income Neighborhoods

Larger supermarkets often provide the best opportunity for accessing affordable, nutritious foods due to greater selections of fresh fruits and vegetables at lower prices. Unfortunately, over time, supermarkets have moved out of low-income urban neighborhoods into more affluent suburbs (Chung and Myers 1999; Weinberg 2000). This lack of large supermarkets is cited as one of the primary barriers to accessing fresh, nutritious, and affordable foods in low-income neighborhoods as well as in neighborhoods of color (Raja et al. 2008).

Philadelphia is no stranger to this problem. A study of Philadelphia by The Food Trust, a nonprofit organization founded in 1992 to ensure that everyone has access to affordable, nutritious food, found that the city had the second lowest number of supermarkets per capita in the country, and that the number of supermarkets in the lowest-income neighborhoods in the Philadelphia region was 156 percent less than in its highest-income neighborhoods. This disinvestment by food retailers carries significant health consequences. Residents in low-income neighborhoods in Philadelphia suffer from a higher incidence of diet-related diseases (Perry 2001). The study by The Food Trust acknowledges that simply increasing the availability of nutritious, affordable foods does not guarantee a reduction in diet-related diseases. However, it notes that "by removing [the] barriers to healthy eating [such as the lack of supermarkets], we can better focus on helping people improve their diets and health" (Perry 2001).

Innovative Financing to Attract Supermarkets

Thanks to the leadership and vision of The Food Trust, Pennsylvania has become a model for how communities can use public-private partnerships to bring food retail back into underserved neighborhoods. Pennsylvania offers gap financing to food retailers in an effort to remove the financial barriers that may limit food retail development in cities. With support from the Commonwealth of Pennsylvania, The Food Trust, the Greater Philadelphia Urban Affairs Coalition, and The Reinvestment Fund (TRF) established a public private partnership to create a financial mechanism to spur grocery store development in underserved neighborhoods in Pennsylvania. Created in 2004, the Pennsylvania Fresh Food Financing Initiative (FFFI) is funded through a state appropriation of $30 million, as well as $90 million from TRF. The $120 million FFFI fund is intended to serve as a one-stop-shop for financing fresh food operators who wish to develop a grocery store in underserved communities where conventional financial institutions may not cover the total costs of infrastructure and necessary credit.

Thanks to the leadership and vision of The Food Trust, Pennsylvania has become a model for how communities can use public-private partnerships to bring food retail back into underserved neighborhoods.

FFFI offers a range of financing options from predevelopment grants to loans. The monies can be used for financing land acquisition and equipment. In addition, supermarkets that plan to develop new stores in underserved communities can also take advantage of an additional $100 million available through the Commonwealth of Pennsylvania's First Industries Program (www.thefoodtrust.org).

Strict eligibility guidelines are in place to ensure that the original intent of FFFI is served. Grocery store operators seeking grant or loan money must demonstrate that the proposed project will benefit an underserved area. An underserved area is defined as "a low- or moderate-income census tract, an area of below-average supermarket density, or an area having a supermarket customer base with more than 50 percent living in a low-income census tract or other area demonstrated to have significant access limitations due to travel distance" (TRF 2004).

To ensure success of the projects, TRF, the organization that manages the financial component of the program, offers technical assistance to its borrowers and grantees. An additional partner, The Greater Philadelphia Urban Affairs Coalition, assists eligible minority- and women-owned businesses in becoming supermarket developers using FFFI funds (www.trf.org).

Since its creation in the fall of 2004, FFFI has funded 50 supermarket projects in areas including Philadelphia, Pittsburgh, Eddystone, and Gettysburg, with a total of more than $38.9 million in grant and loan investment. These 50 new stores represent more than 1.2 million square feet of fresh food retail space and created 3700 new jobs in underserved neighborhoods (Perry 2008). In addition, FFFI staff is currently processing requests for assistance from 67 projects located in urban and rural communities throughout Pennsylvania (Smith 2007a).

Figure 4-13. *A Food 4 Less store funded through the FFFI program in Allentown, Pennyslvania.*

Figure 4-14. *Mastrocco's store funded through the FFFI program in Derry, Pennsylvania.*

SHOP RITE: HEALTHFUL FOODS AND LOCAL ECONOMIC DEVELOPMENT

One of the FFFI-funded stores is Shop Rite located on Island Avenue in the Eastwick section of Philadelphia. The store opened with help from a $5 million FFFI loan for construction and a $250,000 grant by TRF. This redeveloped 57,000-square-foot store has created 258 quality jobs with attractive employee benefits. And these jobs are mostly filled by residents from the surrounding neighborhood.

According to Patricia Smith from TRF, the owner of Shop Rite, Jeff Brown, is committed to providing high-quality customer service as well as contributing to the local community. Because of this, Brown used a substantial portion of the TRF grant money for workforce development and employee training. Thanks to the grant, he was able to train the new employees, many of whom are from the local neighborhood, in customer service to ensure a good experience for the customers (Smith 2007a).

Figure 4-15. Shop Rite store funded through the Fresh FFFI program in Philadelphia.

Stores such as Shop Rite are also playing a larger role in their communities. For example, Shop Rite offers a community room for its customers. It also responds to the cultural preferences of its customers. For instance, Shop Rite's owner, Jeff Brown, observed that a large number of his customers are Muslims, who prefer to eat halal meat (i.e., meat slaughtered according to Islamic tradition). The owner responded by putting pressure on his suppliers to provide halal meat. Patricia Smith from TRF notes the positive impacts of independent stores like Shop Rite:

> [T]hese kinds of locally-owned grocery stores are building bridges between different ethnic and religious groups as well as across income boundaries. There is even talk of using some of the stores as sort of an organizing forum for working class families. Maybe allowing other services to operate in grocery stores, like a tax services table during tax season that is geared particularly for folks with earned income tax credits. These stores are community builders. They can stabilize neighborhoods that have seen rougher times. (Smith 2007a)

In addition to promoting food access, the public-private partnership in Pennsylvania sees the creation of new supermarkets as a means to spur economic development. A recent study contracted by TRF found that "the introduction of a new supermarket increases both the levels and rates of appreciation of home prices near the new store" (TRF 2007). The report also found that supermarket development has the potential to significantly affect employment and earnings. In one case, the development of a grocery store in Philadelphia County is estimated to have increased employment by 660 jobs and increased earnings by $12,466,000 countywide (TRF 2007).

The Healthy Corner Stores Initiative

Many low-income neighborhoods in the U.S. are served by small independent grocery stores. These grocery stores are reported to offer fewer selections of healthful foods, such as fresh fruits and vegetables *(Food for Growth 2003)*. When available, healthful foods tend to be more expensive in these smaller grocery stores. Nonetheless, these small stores offer an extensive food retail network in low-income neighborhoods. As well, these stores are sources of current employment for economically strapped neighborhoods. Scholars (Raja et al. 2008; Short et al. 2007) have argued that, rather than chase after new large supermarkets, it may be more prudent to support existing small grocery stores.

Recognizing the role of these small food retailers in neighborhoods, the Healthy Corner Store Initiative (HSCI) is a program geared to provide financial assistance to small corner grocery stores in making a greater offering of healthful foods in underserved neighborhoods. Also funded through the FFFI initiative, typical projects include funding for an upgrade in refrigeration systems so that corner store operators can stock fruits and vegetables.

The Corner Store Campaign

Along with increasing the supply for healthful foods, it is important to increase the demand for healthful foods. This is especially important for the nation's youth who are at risk of diet-related disease, such as diabetes, due to their eating habits. Researchers estimate that 610 calories of the average teenagers' daily diet comes from snack foods. In Philadelphia, even elementary school students reported they visited corner stores daily, buying mostly junk food. Recognizing this balance between demand for and supply of healthful foods, The Food Trust has embarked on a campaign that "seeks to reduce the incidence of diet-related disease and obesity by improving the snack food choices made by adolescents in corner stores" (www.thefoodtrust.org). The campaign encourages corner stores to increase their availability of healthful foods: participating corner store operators agree to create a section of healthy options in their stores that contains foods with seven grams of fat or less.

Smartly, The Food Trust recognizes it is not enough to just increase availability of healthful foods. The campaign also uses social marketing and education to increase the demand for healthful food. The campaign prepares urban savvy, youth-informed marketing materials in stores and schools to promote healthy eating. It also relies on a leadership team of students called Snack Smart Street Soldiers (S4) that have vowed to make healthier choices and to encourage their peers to do the same. S4 has created their own comic book and informational and motivational trading cards, and made morning public address announcements to inform their peers about eating healthy.

Figures 4-18 to 4-21 (clockwise): Social marketing messages prepared as part of the Healthy Corner Store Campaign promoting healthy eating, water and 100% juice, and smart snacking.

Photos courtesy of The Food Trust

ROMANO'S GROCERY: A CORNER STORE WITH HEALTHFUL FOODS

Figure 4-16. Healthy Corner store-- Romano's grand opening.

Romano's Grocery in Juniata Park neighborhood is a model for increasing healthful food access by building on the assets of the existing food environment. This store has been transformed from a typical corner store selling dry goods, candy, sundries, and a small selection of fresh foods to a "triple-green" business. With funding from FFFI and the Department of Community Economic Development Minority Food Retailer Program, along with support from the William Penn Foundation and TRF's Sustainable Development Fund, the owner renovated the store using green building practices. The renovated store includes energy-efficient lighting and refrigerators that are 25 percent to 35 percent more efficient than standard ones. A ductless HVAC system minimizes the additional energy costs associated with the refrigeration needed to stock fresh fruits and vegetables. Romano's Grocery is able to stock more fresh fruits and vegetables as well as expand its business (Smith 20007b).

Figure 4-17. Corner store displaying a 'smart snacking' advertisement as part of the Healthy Corner Store Campaign.

How Did FFFI Come to Be?

The state-funded FFFI program exists thanks to the systematic research, implementation, and advocacy efforts of The Food Trust. The Food Trust, in collaboration with Philadelphia's Department of Health, began its supermarket campaign efforts in 2001 by researching, publishing, and disseminating information on the relationship between the lack of grocery stores and diet-related diseases in Philadelphia. Following the release of a report, "The Need for More Supermarkets in Philadelphia," a local city councilor, Blondell Reynolds Brown, directed The Food Trust to convene a Food Marketing Task Force. The charge of the Food Marketing Task Force was to develop policy recommendations that would facilitate the availability of nutritious, affordable foods in Philadelphia. Forty experts from the private, public, and civic sectors that included representatives from the supermarket industry and child nutrition advocates convened as a task force. Over a 12-month period, these experts met and developed 10 policy recommendations that city and state officials could implement to increase the amount of supermarket development in Philadelphia (Burton and Perry 2004).

These recommendations were well received by the state legislature and the governor. One legislator in particular, Dwight Evans, became the primary champion for the supermarket campaign. The program also received support from the Pennsylvania House Health and Human Service Committee chaired by Representatives George Kenny and Frank Oliver. The State Assembly recognized that a lack of supermarkets was prolific across the state and that improving food access in underserved communities would not only provide access to healthy food, but also spur economic development by creating jobs in the food retail sector.

TRF, a community development financial organization established in 1985, was identified as the organization that was best equipped to manage the funds for grocery store development. The nonprofit organization has built a strong reputation in the community as a financer and supporter of development projects to "low-wealth communities and low- and moderate-income individuals" (www.trfund.com). According to Patricia Smith, the Director of Special Initiatives at TRF, the elected officials, including Representative Evans, believed that in order to make something successful, dedicated resources were needed. "Often times, government is not the best sector to manage projects like this. Representative Evans understood the need for quality lending in this case, and TRF was positioned well to administer the project" (Smith 2007a). The Reinvestment Fund also offered to match the funding that the state contributed and thus additional funding was leveraged for the project (Smith 2007a).

Lessons for Planners

The FFFI project benefited greatly from The Food Trust's leadership in many ways. The Food Trust generated well-researched evidence to convince policy makers and the community about the scope and impact of the problem (lack of access to healthful foods) and the importance of the solution (supermarket creation).

Duane Perry, the founder of The Food Trust and a planner by training, also attributes of the success of the FFFI process because of the singular focus on supermarket development. The Food Trust also used language directed at policy makers. Describing the manner in which they brought the problem of food access to policy makers, Perry (2007) notes:

> We never termed it food security; we talked only about the lack of grocery stores. We didn't talk about farmers markets or community gardens in those meetings. Those are important, but often times policy makers see them as issues that they don't normally engage in. But supermarkets are something they can engage in and do something about. The lack of supermarkets is easy to understand for a wide range of people.

What led to the subsequent success of the FFFI program? According to Smith (2007a):

> We started by picking the right projects in the beginning. We focused on improving existing supermarkets that we knew would be successful, rather than starting with funding start-ups that we didn't know if they'd succeed. Now that we have some successes under our belt, we can say, "Look, these existing grocery stores have been upgraded, improved, and now carry more nutritious foods." Now we've proven that there is a market for these grocery stores in underserved areas.

Furthermore, a strong component of The Food Trust's efforts (as well as those by TRF) is to monitor and evaluate the successes of their programs and policies in order to learn from them. In 2008, the two organizations are partnering in a study funded by the National Institute of Environmental Health Sciences to evaluate FFFI's impact on diet and healthful eating. Working with the Pennsylvania State University and University of London, the study will compare fruit and vegetable consumption patterns and evaluate whether these patterns change after the opening of a new supermarket.

Planners have a role to play in supermarket location and prevalence by removing barriers, both regulatory and financial, that prevent the private market from establishing food destinations. At a minimum, Duane Perry and David Adler from The Food Trust suggest that planners need to begin by considering food access a planning issue.

> The same way planners ask questions like How are we going to provide good transportation and housing?, they need to also ask, How are people going to get access to food? Even though food retail is part of the private market, it doesn't happen automatically or evenly. Planners can help prioritize food retail and make it a separate issue from where the next clothing store is going to go. (Adler 2007)

Perry further points out the need for intervention and assistance to ensure food destinations and healthy communities for everybody.

> Planning needs to embrace a broader agenda that includes food. Also, planners and policy makers need to find ways to work with the food industry and understand how the industry operates instead of trying to dictate how supermarkets are designed. (Perry 2007)

For example, the use of economic development funds as an incentive for attracting, retaining, or improving food retail, such as through the FFFI project, can simultaneously promote healthful eating as well as economic development in a community.

LOUISVILLE, KENTUCKY: HEALTHFUL FOOD ENVIRONMENTS IN AND AROUND PUBLIC HOUSING SITES

On a sunny Saturday morning in late summer, rural Kentucky farmers sell their produce against the backdrop of a brightly colored mural. Fresh arugula, green peppers, and plum tomatoes are piled high on tables. Shoppers watch

Planners have a role to play in supermarket location and prevalence by removing barriers, both regulatory and financial, that prevent the private market from establishing food destinations.

Figure 4-22. Smoketown–Shelby Park farmers' market.

Jessica Kozlowski Russell

Figure 4-23. Chef Nancy shows shoppers at the farmers' market tasty ways to prepare the vegetables available at the market.

Active Living by Design

Chef Nancy cooking rutabagas and spinach. Balloons and a smartly designed sign welcome people to the Smoketown-Shelby Park farmers' market.

It would be easy to imagine such a scene in an upscale neighborhood. But lavish houses or upscale condos do not surround this market. This thriving farmers' market, which began in 2004, is located in a middle school parking lot adjacent to Sheppard Square, a 325-unit public housing complex operated by the Metro Louisville Housing Authority within a low-income neighborhood in Louisville's East Downtown area. Customers here can use an EBT card, WIC tokens, or their senior farmers' market vouchers to purchase the locally grown and healthful produce. One block away from the market, kids weed and harvest tomatoes grown in a community garden located in the heart of the Smoketown Neighborhood surrounded by the Sheppard Square housing complex. These food destinations—especially, the farmers' market—are a lush oasis in a relative food desert, allowing residents direct access to fresh, local produce. This case study documents the trajectory of these efforts by a coalition of government and nongovernmental agencies to improve the neighborhood food environments for public housing and low-income residents in East Downtown, Louisville.

Poor Food Access for Public Housing Residents in East Downtown

East Downtown Louisville has its share of challenges. The area, which is located approximately only six blocks east of the Louisville's central business district, is comprised of three neighborhoods, Phoenix Hill, Smoketown, and Shelby Park, aligned north to south, with the Ohio River forming the northern boundary and Interstate 65 forming the western boundary. The Interstate acts as a barrier, isolating the area from other parts of the city.

In addition to challenges due to its urban form, like many inner-city areas, East Downtown is poor and has a high percentage of racial minorities. The median annual household income is only $14,333, well below that of its host Jefferson County ($39,457). Of its 10,224 residents, 68 percent (6,971) are African-American (CFA 2007). The area is also home to several public housing residents. In Smoketown, the neighborhood containing the Smoketown–Shelby farmers' market, 42 percent of the residents reside in the Sheppard Square public housing complex (CFA 2007). In the Phoenix Hill neighborhood is another public housing project, the Clarksdale project, a 700-unit public housing complex covering 30 acres. This complex is currently being demolished and redeveloped into Liberty Green through the federal Housing Opportunities for People Everywhere (HOPE VI) public housing program.

The Problem: Inadequate Food Environments in East Downtown

The residents in East Downtown are food insecure. In 2004, the Community Farm Alliance,[5] a nonprofit organization, began a community food assessment process to judge the quality and access to food in East Downtown.[6] An interim report from the assessment notes that "residents of low-income…East Downtown areas are likely to have to spend the most to buy foods and have the least access to high-quality foods" (CFA 2007). The community lacks large food retailers that typically provide a variety of food at reasonable prices. The convenience stores and discount stores located in the community offer foods of lower quality (CFA 2007). Unfortunately, independent grocery stores too lack the capacity to offer high-quality goods and services. Shoppers at one independent grocery store located within walking distance of East Downtown, for example, are accosted by unpleasant odors emanating from a meat processing plant located in its basement. The visual cues in the store add to an unwelcoming shopping experience: a sign announces, "Warning, shoplifters will be arrested."

Figures 4-24 to 4-26. This store in East Downtown sells mostly processed food (e.g., a whole aisle of Ramen noodles) and red meats, with no produce or other healthful offerings for area residents; a warning sign makes for an unfriendly food shopping environment.

From a public health perspective, the problem of the lack of healthful food destinations in East Downtown is exacerbated by the abundance of fast-food restaurants. On Broadway Ave, a main thoroughfare running through and connecting East Downtown with West Louisville, 24 fast-food restaurants lie along a 2.8-mile stretch. Residents in these neighborhoods are never more than one-tenth of a mile away from the nearest fast-food chain, while superstores or grocery stores are out of reach. Given the accessibility of fast-food restaurants, it is hardly surprising that a study of youth at area middle schools revealed that 60 percent of students eat one or more fast-food meals per day, and some eat up to three fast-food meals per day (CFA 2007).

This food environment—marked by a lack of access to fresh healthful foods and the abundance of fast foods—is especially limiting for residents who do not own vehicles to drive to food stores outside of their neighborhoods. A majority (51 percent) of the households in East Downtown do not have access to a vehicle, and in some neighborhoods within East Downtown, that figure is 70 percent (CFA 2007).

The Actors and Institutions: Unusual Partnerships to Improve Food Environments

An unusual partnership of government organizations and government agencies has paved the way for improving the neighborhood food environment in East Downtown, especially for residents living in public housing. In 2003, the Louisville Metro Government and the Louisville Metro Housing Authority founded ACTIVE Louisville (AL), a partnership dedicated to "creat[ing] more vibrant neighborhoods where residents incorporate healthy habits into their daily routine." The program, which receives funding support from the Robert Wood Johnson Foundation, initiated a partnership of multiple local government agencies and nonprofits to ensure that Liberty Green, the new redeveloped public housing project, provides opportunities for physi-

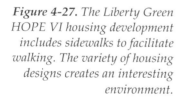

Figure 4-27. The Liberty Green HOPE VI housing development includes sidewalks to facilitate walking. The variety of housing designs creates an interesting environment.

Jessica Kozlowski Russell

cal activity for public housing residents as well as for people living in the neighborhood. The redevelopment plan includes proposals for active living design components, such as "pocket parks, a walkable streetscape, and an active living center for the community" (www.activelivingbydesign.org).

At its inception, improving food environments was not part of AL's mission. Nonetheless, very quickly, the AL partnership recognized that creating a healthy environment includes ensuring access to nutritious, affordable, and culturally appropriate foods. As a result, in 2004, a year after its creation, AL expanded its mission to include efforts to improve the food environment in its target neighborhoods. AL fulfills this mission by collaborating with several partners within and outside the local government. Within the local government structure, AL's efforts are aligned with the "Healthy Hometown Movement," an initiative spearheaded by the mayor's office to demonstrate city government's interest in encouraging people to lead healthier, more active lives and to make healthier choices. The Louisville Public Health and Wellness Department and its Center for Health Equity play an integral role in policy initiatives.

Within the larger community, AL collaborates with organizations and individuals with a rich understanding of and experience with improving local food security; these include, among others, the Community Farm Alliance, a local chef, local schools, and community centers.

As described below, the collective efforts of these partners have resulted in tangible improvements in the neighborhood food environment, and perhaps more importantly, made visible the importance of addressing the issue of healthful food and healthy eating for public housing residents.

It is not enough to merely provide the fresh food. It must also be affordable to residents. To address this, the farmers' market accepts EBT cards, WIC Nutrition Coins, and Seniors Farmers' Market Nutrition (SFMNP) vouchers.

The Solutions

Through the AL partnership, local governments in Louisville worked to improve the food environments for East Downtown residents in several ways.

Locating farmers' markets in and around public housing sites and lower-income neighborhoods. Today, public housing and other residents of East Downtown access nutritious, affordable food at the Smoketown-Shelby Park Farmers' market. The farmers' market operates every Saturday from June through October in the Meyzeek Middle School parking lot, directly across the street from public housing. The farmers' market is within walking distance of three public housing sites: Sheppard Park, Liberty Green (being built to replace the Clarksdale public housing site), and Dosker Manner, a senior public housing site. The school location for the farmers' market was secured due to a relationship that existed between the Community Center and the principal of the school. The school supports the idea of a permanent space for the market on its grounds, even allowing a mural to be painted with the help of local residents to create a designated space for the market.

However, it is not enough to merely provide the fresh food. It must also be affordable to residents. To address this, the farmers' market accepts EBT cards, WIC Nutrition Coins, and Seniors Farmers' Market Nutrition (SFMNP) vouchers. The SFMNP program is a statewide program that allots seniors with incomes less than 185 percent of the Federal Poverty Income Guidelines $40 a year to purchase fruits and vegetables from participating farmer's markets. The $40 allotment comes in the form of $2 vouchers and can be used only for the purchase of locally grown fruits and vegetables. Farmers need only to apply for a free license, attend a brief training session, and then post their license during the farmers market. The $2 vouchers that farmers receive are deposited into their personal accounts similarly to a check.

*Figure 4-28 (left). Residents using Senior Farmers' Market Nutrition Vouchers at the farmers' market. **Figure 4-29** (below). Sheppard Park Public Housing next to St. Peter Claver's Community Garden.*

The market also allows recipients of food stamps to use their EBT card to buy produce. The market has an EBT card reader that allows the customer to select their produce and "check out" with the market manager where the card is swiped. At end of the day, the market manager provides a check directly to the farmers based on their sales throughout the day. The Department of Health and Wellness contributed to the partnership by paying for the EBT card reader.

In 2005, the market served 1,900 customers, half of which were low-income residents (CFA 2007). Part of the markets' success is owed to the high level of organization. The manager operates an ad hoc bank for the market, making it easy for the 10 farmers to participate in the low-income voucher systems. The manager position is supported through a grant from a local bank. The Presbyterian Community Center acts as the fiscal agent for the farmers' market and the Friends of the Smoketown/Shelby Park Farmers' Market form its oversight committee.

Recipients of WIC support can also participate in the farmers' market thanks to a grant by the Robert Wood Johnson Foundation's Healthy Eating by Design program and Friends of the Shelby/Smoketown Farmers' Market. The funding is used to provide WIC recipients with money to purchase fruits and vegetables.[7] Residents receiving WIC vouchers must just sign their name to register, and they receive $10 in wooden coins to cover the purchases. At the end of the day, the farmers cash out the coins at the market's bank. At the end of the 2005 season, the market supported 200 WIC recipients, and the market hopes to leverage these results to encourage the program's implementation in the future (CFA 2007).

Locating community gardens within public housing projects. With a successful farmers' market underway, AL focused its attention on creating an interactive community garden within the Sheppard Square public housing site. The idea for St. Peter Claver Garden was not initially inspired by the desire to provide access to healthy food, but rather to address a more familiar planning problem: vacant land. Urban Design Associates, a planning and architecture firm from Boston, was charged with preparing the Master Plan for Smoketown neighborhood. It proposed establishing community gardens in areas of unusable land called "soft middles." Soft middles are the result of the original street grid design that created large superblocks with alleyways that left land in the middle unused and unclaimed by property owners. These soft middles are not suitable to build new housing or large enough to add new streets and thus remain empty space. One such soft middle was owned by the Louisville Metro Housing Authority.

While the Metro Housing Authority was supportive of the community garden idea, the organization did not see the operation of the garden as being within its mission. Instead the Housing Authority, under the leadership of AL, drew on its partnerships to support the mission and eventual operation of the community garden. The lot owned by the Housing Authority was deeded to Louisville's land bank to make it eligible for the city's liability coverage. Then the Presbyterian Community Center, which works closely with the Housing Authority and AL, became the lease holding agency. Finally, AL took responsibility for the maintenance and management of the garden through a memorandum of understanding with the Presbyterian Community Center. With financial support from the Healthy Eating by Design grant, and $70,000 worth of bio-remediation from the Metro Government of Louisville, the garden was established as the St. Peter Claver's Community Garden.

St. Peter Claver's Community Garden formed in 2006. The half-acre site located within the Sheppard Park public housing development is home to 15 garden plots. Gardeners grow produce and vegetables. Initially, the garden was intended for nearby senior residents. The gardens received a lukewarm reception from seniors, however, while other groups, including children and educators at Meyzeek Middle School, were far more interested in gardening. Three groups of students from Meyzeek middle school currently use the garden: an after-school program; a local foundation targeting chronically truant children; and a gardening club, sponsored by an ecology/science teacher. Additional nonprofit organizations, such as a food literacy program and the Presbyterian Community Center, use the garden to do educational programming with children about agriculture in an attempt to reintroduce urban youth to the origin of their food.

Figure 4-30. Entrance to St. Peter Claver's Community Garden.

Figure 4-31 (center). School children gardening at St. Peter Claver's Community Garden. Figure 4-32 (below). St. Peter Claver's Community Garden.

An additional one-time grant of $30,000 from the Metro Sewer Authority supported the community garden. The grant was part of the Sewer Authority's Consent Decree, which requires them to develop landscapes that reduce stormwater runoff. The grant was used to build two rain gardens and to acquire rain barrels to collect rain water for watering plants. The grant has also paid for the garden entrance, which includes native plants, and a pavilion for classes. The grant also supports a staff position and staff assistance for continual landscaping.

Enhancing transportation access to food for seniors. Given the challenge of low automobile ownership rates and physical limitations among seniors, AL facilitated an innovative transportation option for senior residents residing in East Downtown with no access to a car. Once a month, usually corresponding to the time of food stamp disbursement, a bus takes seniors on a Saturday morning shopping trip. The bus, which is provided by the local grocery store, stops at the farmers' market for fresh produce and then goes to the grocery store so seniors can buy other food items, such as canned and frozen foods.

Because people's choice to consume healthful foods is influenced by their knowledge of health and nutrition, AL arranges for a nutritionist from the local extension service to accompany the seniors on the bus. The nutritionist provides seniors with information about the price of foods at the grocery store and farmers' market to make easier comparison shopping for more healthful foods.[8]

The Future: Turning Food Destination Projects into Powerful Policy and Supporting Citywide Efforts

AL's efforts have evolved from focusing only on physical activity to increasing access to healthful food destinations and community gardens. Efforts have further evolved to include policy development. The Food Security Task Force (FSTF) was formed in 2007 to address the systematic, environmental, and policy-based barriers that restrain efforts at healthy eating. The task force was convened by the Center for Healthy Equity (part of Metro Louisville's Public Health and Wellness Department), the Community Farm Alliance, and AL as a food policy initiative. The task force also includes community members, government agencies, the private sector, and nonprofit organizations. In its initial stages, the group has defined three key activities:

1. To systematically analyze geographically and economically marginalized communities to understand contextual barriers to healthy eating.

2. To raise awareness of food insecurity in the community and inform residents on the best practices to address these barriers , including market-based, policy, and regulatory solutions.

3. To use their findings and community base to develop a set of policy recommendations and advocate for changes to eliminate systemic barriers to healthy eating in underserved neighborhoods.

Although still in the beginning stages of an action plan, the group has identified some possible policy initiatives , including: creating incentives for corner stores to stock locally grown, healthy foods; the development of major retail outlets in underserved areas; expanding farmers' markets; expanding the WIC and Senior Farmers' Market Nutrition Program; and increasing job opportunities in low-income areas.

Given the challenge of low automobile ownership rates and physical limitations among seniors, AL facilitated an innovative transportation option for senior residents residing in East Downtown with no access to a car.

As part of AL's efforts to increase the scale of the healthy eating program to the city level, it recognizes existing efforts by other organizations. In West Louisville, it supports the work of three partner organizations in promoting a neighborhood farmers' market. The California Farmers' Market began operation in February 2007 and is operated by Urban Fresh[9] in partnership with the Community Farm Alliance and the Muhammad Ali Institute.

Figure 4-33. *Sign at Victory Park Farmers' Market.*

AL is also supportive of a new food distribution center created in West Louisville by the Community Farm Alliance. Grasshopper's Distribution is a farmer-owned distribution center that connects food retailers to local farmers. Each week, the distribution center staff contacts food retailers and area farmers to determine what food is needed, what is available, and to negotiate prices between the two parties. Grasshoppers Distribution staff then travel to area farms to pick up produce and deliver it their client base–food retailers.

Figure 4-34. *Fresh locally grown produce at Grasshoppers' Distribution waiting to be delivered to area restaurants.*

Finally, AL and its partners' efforts have gotten the attention of other city agencies, such as Metro's Economic Development Department. According to Sarah Howard of the Louisville Metro Housing Authority, the Economic Development Department is beginning to see food retail as a possible economic development and neighborhood stabilization strategy. Accordingly, the Economic Development Department has committed resources to commission two studies: "Regional Farmers Market Feasibility Study" and a "Retail Infrastructure Analysis." The "Farmers Market Feasibility Study" will determine if the Louisville region can support a year-round, indoor farmers' market. The department is commissioning the "Retail Infrastructure Analysis" to examine and better understand the food retail environment.

Lessons for Planners

Louisville chose a variety of innovative solutions to address the lack of healthful foods in and around public housing locations. AL also has plans to take its programs to the citywide scale instead of neighborhoods. But little has been done to address the systemic failures causing food insecurity and food inequities in the city, many of which—such as economic inequality—may be beyond the scope of the organization. The Food Security Task Force, however, is a step in the right direction.

Include food retail when planning new public housing. The new HOPE VI public housing development includes some provision for retail space, but no plans are in place to attract conventional food retail or to provide incentives to attract corner stores that will provide healthful foods. This is a missed opportunity. HOPE VI funds from HUD cannot be used for retail space, but another federal program, the New Market Tax Credit program, is being used to fund the retail development. Due to the limited amount of available space, commercial uses in Liberty Green will likely be devoted to office space and services, such as banks and a post office. As of yet, no efforts have been made to encourage food retail. Sarah Howard of the Louisville Metro Housing Authority indicates that AL partners would like to see food retail included in Liberty Green but doubts that this will happen. She also questions if a large grocery store is the right fit for an otherwise dense, walkable neighborhood. Alternatively attracting small food stores, such as bodegas or corner stores, might increase access to food (Raja et al., 2008; Short et al. 2007), but Howard remains concerned that this increased access often comes at a higher price and is not always healthier. Nonetheless, Liberty Green's major redesign provides a great opportunity to pursue the possibility of including a year-round neighborhood healthful food destination within the housing development.

Partnerships among local government agencies and nonprofit organizations can transform food environments, especially in low-income neighborhoods. The Louisville case demonstrates that the leadership of and partnership among local government agencies and nonprofit organizations can transform food environments in low-income and underserved communities, especially in and around public housing sites. Local government agencies, including the Metro Housing Authority, the Sewer Authority, and the Health Departments, play a critical role by providing resources and removing barriers to projects. Having a supportive mayor and city council that raised the salience of healthy eating and healthy living helped as well. Nonprofit organizations, such as the Community Farm Alliance, are a major force in sustaining the healthy eating efforts in the Louisville area by generating information and engaging in advocacy work. Communities can turn to Louisville as an example of how to enliven and improve food environments in and around neighborhoods where public housing is or may be located in the future.

PORTLAND, OREGON: USING A FOOD POLICY COUNCIL TO PROMOTE HEALTHY EATING

On the second Wednesday of each month, Portland, Oregon, community members convene to discuss issues of food access, urban gardening, land preservation, sustainability, farmers' markets, and people's consumption

The new HOPE VI public housing development includes some provision for retail space, but no plans are in place to attract conventional food retail or to provide incentives to attract corner stores that will provide healthful foods. This is a missed opportunity.

of nutritious, local food. Among those in attendance are a chef, physician, lawyer, farmer, anti-hunger advocate, university representative, government official, and a restaurant owner. The group, the Portland/Multnomah Food Policy Council (PMFPC), was created in 2002 to advise government agencies about city and county food-related issues.

The PMFPC vision is to ensure that "all city of Portland and Multnomah County residents have access to a wide variety of nutritious, affordable, and culturally appropriate food" through a mix of demonstration projects in the community, collecting and disseminating research, and advocating for the inclusion of food-related issues in the planning process and city documents. The council is comprised of individuals or representatives from community groups as well as representatives from Portland's Metro government, and staff members from the City of Portland Office of Sustainable Development and Multnomah County Sustainability and Public Health Departments. Among the council's accomplishments are a community food assessment (CFA) in a low-income neighborhood, a series of reports indicating suitable places for urban agriculture, institutional purchases of local foods in the county's corrections system, and involvement in Portland's comprehensive plan update.

This case study follows the evolution of the PMFPC and the role that a FPC can play in ensuring long-term access to nutritious, affordable food.

Context

Portland is located in Oregon on the northern edge of the fertile Willamette Valley. Its location near the confluence of the Willamette and Columbia Rivers made Portland a popular place among early settlers for trade and agricultural reasons. Today, the city of Portland is home to roughly 530,000 people and the Portland metropolitan area contains about 2 million people. Eighty-seven percent of Portland residents are white. According to the 2000 census, the median family income is $40,146; 8.5 percent of families live below the poverty line.

Farming has a strong history in Oregon. It became a major part of the state's economy in the 1830s. Early settlers recognized that the fertile soil and mild climate was well suited to fruit, berry, and vegetable cultivation as well as the rearing of livestock. Today, approximately 28 percent (17.1 million acres) of Oregon's land is in agriculture use, and agriculture-related activity accounts for 10 percent of Oregon's gross state product and more than 150,000 jobs. The agricultural base is diverse with roughly 220 different crops grown throughout the state along with many varieties of livestock. Many farms have long been part of Oregon's cultural history. More than 1,000 family farms and ranches in Oregon claim the distinction of being century farms—that is, having been owned by the same family for more than 100 years (ODA 2007).

Oregon was an early adopter of state growth management regulation to preserve farmland and prevent urban development on agricultural land adjacent to urban areas. State land-use controls include urban growth boundaries (UGBs), the first of which was created in 1979. UGBs were put into place around urbanized areas statewide in an effort to preserve existing farmland from urban expansion and speculative buying. Oregon also developed exclusive farm use (EFU) zoning that permits only agriculture and agricultural-related activities in EFU-zoned rural areas. EFU zoning defines minimum lot size for farmland and ranchland as 80 and 160 acres, respectively (ODA 2007a).

In part due to the state's actions to regulate urban growth, Oregon has a reputation for leadership in issues of sustainability, global warming, and environmental preservation. In Portland, efforts to preserve the environment,

Today, approximately 28 percent (17.1 million acres) of Oregon's land is in agriculture use, and agriculture-related activity accounts for 10 percent of Oregon's gross state product and more than 150,000 jobs.

Protecting farmland is only one big food system challenge in Oregon; hunger is another. In 2002, findings from the Center on Hunger and Poverty of Brandeis University indicated that 14.3 percent of Oregon households were food insecure and 6.2 percent were food insecure with hunger.

manage waste, and use alternative energy are integrated and directed by the Office of Sustainable Development. This institutional groundwork provides a good footing for the food system work of PMFPC.

The Problem

Despite the successes of land-use regulations, farmland is in jeopardy as development pressures persist. The Portland area suffers from a common problem faced by many urban areas. Prime farmland is most susceptible to development pressures: "Seventy percent of Oregon's highest quality soils are in the Willamette Valley where more than 70 percent of the state's population resides and where population growth pressures are sure to increase" (ODA 2007a).

UGBs were in place for almost 25 years until a citizen referendum, Measure 37, was adopted in 2005. Known generally as "pay or waive" legislation, Measure 37 forced a local government to either waive land-use regulations that prevented development or to pay for the loss of property value. Measure 37 reversed the measures that were put in place to protect farmland and allowed farmland to be developed under the regulations that existed prior to the creation of UGBs. Under Measure 37, the only way local governments can stop development of land is by compensating landowners for the loss value they would have received if the land was developed. Of the more than 2,000 Measure 37 claims filed by January 2007, two-thirds were filed with state and local government entities to develop farmland (ODA 2007a).

More recently, a new measure was passed to strike a balance between the realities of development pressure and the need to protect farmland. In November 2007, Measure 49 was adopted to modify Measure 37. Measure 49 ensures that "Oregon law provides just compensation for unfair burdens while retaining Oregon's protections for farm and forest uses and the state's water resources" (DLCD 2008). Although Measure 49 reinstates agricultural protection through land controls, development pressures persist as Portland expects see an influx of a million people over the next 20 years (Cohen 2007).

Protecting farmland is only one big food system challenge in Oregon; hunger is another. In 2002, findings from the Center on Hunger and Poverty of Brandeis University indicated that 14.3 percent of Oregon households were food insecure and 6.2 percent were food insecure with hunger.[10] In terms of hunger prevalence, this made Oregon the worst state in the country. Simultaneously, 54 percent of Multnomah County residents were found to be overweight or obese. The diminished access to nutritious affordable food is a key factor in seemingly contradictory issues plaguing Oregon—hunger and obesity (PMFPC 2003).

These challenges are being addressed through a number of grassroots programmatic responses. The Portland Multnomah County area has 16 successful farmers' markets. Community gardens are prevalent and well-used, with residents often placed on a waiting list. The area's anti-hunger community is active, offering a variety of emergency programs to address the daily nutritional needs of the hungry. Other grassroots activities included the formation of a Portland Community Gardens group, a "buy local" movement popularized by the formation of a chain of high-quality markets with local and sustainable purchasing goals (the New Seasons Markets), and an increase in interest in urban agriculture and CSA farms. Until 2002, these programs operated with little coordination, though they shared similar challenges (Briggs 2007).

How the Council Was Created

In 2002, the efforts of multiple community groups coalesced under PMFPC. The creation of the council is the result of collaborative efforts between community groups and a Portland City Commissioner, Dan Saltzman. In 2000, Saltzman, a champion of sustainability, attended an annual forum hosted by the Ecumenical Ministries of Oregon (EMO), "A Place at the Table," at which community groups gathered to discuss the intersections between sustainability, agricultural vitality, and access to nutritious food (Cordello 2007). A result of the forum was a proposal to explore the creation of a FPC as a permanent institution to facilitate collaboration among food groups and to provide policy input to government officials. A steering committee spent the next two years studying other FPC to create a set of guiding principles. In May of 2002, the PMFPC was established as a subcommittee of the Portland/Multnomah County Sustainable Development Commission, a bureau managed by Commissioner Saltzman. The PMFPC became an officially recognized advisory council with the passage of Resolution 02-093 before the Board of Commissioners for Multnomah County, and Resolution 36074 (sponsored by Saltzman) by the Portland City Common Council (Cordello 2007).

How the Council Functions

PMFPC is officially charged with:

> providing input and advice on City and County food-related issues; on implementing the priorities identified in the FPCs annual reports; and in reporting annually to City Council and County Board on FPC progress, work plan, and funding status (City of Portland, Resolution No. 36074).

The council has 18 members, each of whom serves a two-year term with the option to be reappointed for a total of two terms. PMFPC members are appointed jointly by a county and a city commissioner from a pool of applicants. Members represent a wide variety of interests, such as nonprofit organizations, hunger advocates, community gardeners, farmers, restaurateurs, university affiliates, and Metro, the regional planning body for the greater Portland region. The diversity of expertise across the membership is designed to ensure that the council is able to carry out its broad mandate.

Figure 4-35. Portland-Multnomah Food Policy Forum meeting.

Portland Office of Sustainable Development

PMFPC benefits from staff support from Portland's Office of Sustainable Development as well as the Multnomah Sustainable Development Commission. These staff members, one from each office are appointed to work on PMFPC-related work as part of their agency tasks. The time commitment

The Land Use Committee is supported by the community gardens subcommittee that is working with Portland's Parks and Recreation Department to increase funding for education, access, and planning of additional community gardens.

for PMFPC-related tasks of the city staff varies, but the county staff member commits approximately five hours per week to FPC-related work (Cohen 2007).

The Council conducts its policy and advisory work through a series of committees and subcommittees. The three primary committees are: Food Access, Land Use, and Institutional Purchasing. The Food Access Committee is charged with developing community-based solutions to address inadequate food access. The committee works toward this goal with support from three subcommittees: the urban agriculture subcommittee focuses on edible landscapes as a form of urban agriculture; the community foods programs subcommittee seeks to increase resources from and participation in local, state, and federal assistance program such as WIC and EBT programs; and the community food planning subcommittee works on comprehensive plan amendments and CFAs.

The Land Use Committee focuses on the nexus between land-use planning and food issues. One goal of the Land Use Committee is to make policy recommendations on two planning initiatives, the New Look and the Big Look—plans to accommodate growth and revise land-use policies in response to anticipated population growth. Additionally, the Land Use Committee facilitates the Diggable City and Diggable County reports (discussed in the next section). The Land Use Committee is supported by the community gardens subcommittee that is working with Portland's Parks and Recreation Department to increase funding for education, access, and planning of additional community gardens.

The Institutional Purchasing Committee is working on two initiatives to refine the city and county model purchasing language, and to develop a preference policy for local foods that does not interfere with local government policies. The committee is also attempting to get a major food service provider to purchase sustainable, local, organic, low-carbon-footprint foods.

Accomplishments of the Portland/Multnomah Food Policy Council
PMFPC has a broad and holistic mission:

> [B]ringing together a diverse array of stakeholders to integrate the aspects of the food system (production, distribution, access, consumption, processing, and recycling) in order to enhance the environmental, economic, social and nutritional health of the City of Portland and Multnomah County. (Portland 2007)

It works to achieve this mission through pilot projects, working closely with government agencies to include food issues in the planning process, and by producing and dissemination information about food issues to effect policy change.

Generating and distributing information about local food planning and policy issues.
One of PMFPC's most significant contributions has been facilitating and supporting research initiatives about food issues. These include:

- The Diggable City initiatives;

- The Farm Direct Marketing Reports;

- A study of barriers and opportunities to the use of regional and sustainable food products by local institutions;

- the Spork Report, a feasibility analysis on institutional purchases of local food; and

- a report about local food purchases by schools for school lunches.

The Diggable City initiative resulted in a series of reports that provide a comprehensive inventory of city lands suitable for agriculture. Diggable City I took shape when PMFPC collaborated with graduate students from Portland State University's Urban and Regional Planning program; the city bureaus of Water, Parks, and Environmental Services; the Office of Transportation; and Commissioner Saltzman's office. In the first phase, the students worked with these city bureaus to identify 430 individual tax parcels in 289 locations citywide that were suitable to grow food. The land-use database is continuously updated and refined, and is now in its third phase (Diggable City III). The initiative has been expanded to include all Multnomah County available tillable land, resulting in a forthcoming a Diggable County report.

The Farm-Direct Marketing Reports document the activities and recommendations of workshops conducted with immigrant farmers. In these workshops, farmers were assisted in developing business skills in direct sales through building customer relations and understanding what customers like to buy. In addition, the workshops discussed land availability and micro-enterprise financing options. The workshops provide a unique opportunity for government agencies, businesses, and nonprofit organizations to interact with farmers of diverse ethnic backgrounds. The farm-direct marketing information reports are published in multiple languages.

In 2003, PMFPC and a nonprofit group, Community Food Matters, collaborated to produce a study of barriers and opportunities to the use of local, sustainable foods in institutional food service programs. The researchers surveyed institutional purchasers, growers, food processors, and produce distributors to gauge the level of interest in using locally produced food and to document current efforts to that end. The results of the 27 interviews revealed that institutional purchasers estimated that 25 percent of the food they purchase is grown or processed in the Oregon-Washington Region. All interviewees indicated a high level of interest in buying more local food, but common barriers were noted: price, corporate contracts or prime vendor agreements, and uncertain demand (Pierson 2003).

In June 2005, the institutional purchasing committee of PMFPC was presented with the Spork Report, a feasibility analysis about institutional purchases of local food conducted by Portland State University students in support of PMFPC efforts. "The initial research goal was to look at the feasibility and strategies for Portland Public Schools (PPS) to increase the amount of local food purchasing by the nutrition services program and make recommendations to the Food Policy Council" (Adair 2005). The report called on the Portland Public School system to continue a farm-to-school pilot project, to require food distributors to identify product origin, and to craft new local and sustainable purchasing language for future purchasing RFPs (Adair 2005).

One year later, a follow-up report, called Local Lunches, was prepared by Portland State University students for presentation to PMFPC. The report built on the Spork Report, but focused more narrowly on actions steps for initiating farm to cafeteria programs across Oregon (Anderson 2006).

Community food assessment. In 2004, PMFPC undertook a CFA in the Lents community, a low-income, physically isolated area of the city. Although PMFPC primarily focuses on policy initiatives, members viewed the Lents CFA project as an important demonstration project that other community groups could replicate. PMFPC members also felt the assessment could shed light on the poorly understood (by the general public) issue of food access and inequality. The CFA was made possible by partnering with Healthy Eating by Design, a community partnership funded by the Robert Wood

The Diggable City initiative resulted in a series of reports that provide a comprehensive inventory of city lands suitable for agriculture.

Johnson Foundation, and community members in the Lents neighborhood. Through the food assessment, residents identified three primary community needs: a strong desire to have a farmers' market in the Lents neighborhood; the ability to grow food in the Lents community; and the desire to learn to purchase and cook healthy foods on a tight budget.

The issues identified through the Lents CFA resulted in the formation of

Figure 4-36. Community garden in the Lents neighborhood.

the Lents Food Group. A collaboration of the Lents Food Group, Friends of Zenger Farms, Healthy Eating by Design Portland, the Oregon Food Bank, PMFPC, and others helped to identify projects that would assist the neighborhood in meeting their goals and becoming more food secure. An international farmers' market (that is, a farmers' market that features foods common to other countries, often grown and sold by immigrant and refugee farmers) was proposed as one possible solution. Many Lents residents live on a tight budget and grow their own food. The international farmer's market in the Lents increases access to healthy and culturally desired fresh foods, and supports the ethnic diversity of the community residents. Locating a permanent space for the international farmer's market is a goal of the PMFPC.

Figure 4-37. A sign for the Lents farmers' market.

The Lents community received a four-year, $100,000 grant through the Alliance for the Promotion of Physical Activity and Nutrition (APPAN) program, which expanded healthy eating and active living program and began investigating corresponding policy solutions to further improve food access for underserved population groups like those in the Lents neighborhood.

Institutional Purchasing Successes

As a result of collaboration between the Multnomah County Sustainability Initiative and the PMFPC, the Multnomah County penitentiary system piloted a local purchasing project in 2004. The County Sheriff's office spent about $57,000 (about 35 to 55 percent of their total food expenditures) to purchase produce from local Oregon and Southwest Washington farms. Subsequently in 2005, the Sherriff's office revised its food purchasing guideline. The 2005 RFP included sustainability criteria that promotes purchase of local foods. The contractor, Aramark, plans to track local purchases of fresh produce, frozen produce, and dairy and eggs. The RFP language is being revised because the vendor did not include sustainability criteria in their submitted proposal. The Multnomah County Sustainability Initiative convened a stakeholders meeting with the vendor to reinvigorate the pilot project effort for 2007 to ensure sustainability is incorporated as a central focus of the food services specifications in the forthcoming contract revision.

The institutional purchasing committee of PMFPC is currently encouraging additional city and county government offices to adopt directives that will mandate the purchase of locally grown, low-carbon footprint foods for institutional purposes.

Policy Recommendations to Inform the Upcoming Comprehensive Plan Updates

A Metro 2040 plan was created in 1994 to address the anticipated arrival of an additional million people to the Portland Metropolitan area. In 2006, a new plan called the New Look was created as planners realized that population projections indicated that those 1 million people would likely arrive in Portland as early as 2020. For the New Look, planners sought the FPC's advice about how to integrate food system considerations in the new plan.

As Portland revises its comprehensive plan, PMFPC is drafting language to include food security issues. The updated comprehensive plan will include 18 statewide goals, six of which require major updates or revisions. In the pre-planning phase, six technical working groups have been created to address the six categories that need to be revised. One of those six is sustainability; it is here that food system planning, regional food systems, and food security will be addressed. The sustainability working group, which includes planners and members from the water bureau, transportation bureau, and economic bureau, is currently debating what specific food issues need to be addressed in the two-year comprehensive plan revision process. Their efforts will center around collecting data, identifying resources, and deciding on the key questions planners need to address. The end product will be a section in the comprehensive plan that addresses food access, the food economy, farmland preservation, and strategies for protecting farmers as key areas.

Lessons for Planners

Reflecting on the experiences of PMFPC, Suzanne Briggs, one of the original PMFPC members, observes that many people who serve on a FPC aren't necessarily trained in policy-making. She notes:

> We weren't taught policy 101. Most of us on the council were doers. We came to the council as program directors and were thus focused on on-the-ground solutions. We had to always step back and say, okay, but what are the corresponding policies to support this. (Briggs 2007)

In the pre-planning phase, six technical working groups have been created to address the six categories that need to be revised. One of those six is sustainability; it is here that food system planning, regional food systems, and food security will be addressed.

The Food for Growth *authors found that "food items in the West Side were on average more costly" and that "food was found to be closer to expiration in stores on the West Side than the same food items found in chain stores."*

Nonetheless, PMFPC members accomplished a number of policy-related and programmatic tasks. What has made PMFPC successful also presents a key challenge to its future success. It began as a policy-oriented effort but also took on programmatic activities.

FPCs have to balance the policy making, which typically yields benefits in the long run, with the need to engage in activities that offer quick benefits and therefore appeal to people. An effective FPC will have to carefully navigate the two roles of a policy-making body and a program/implementation entity.

The city of Portland and Multnomah County had many disparate programs addressing issues of hunger, healthy eating, and food security. The creation of PMFPC emerged as a mechanism for these groups to collaborate and to affect policy to support food security and healthy eating. PMFPC has been successful in advocating for the inclusion of food in traditional planning efforts.

BUFFALO, NEW YORK: EMPOWERING YOUTH TO TRANSFORM URBAN FOOD ENVIRONMENTS AND NEIGHBORHOODS

As the leaves begin to change color and the days get shorter, a group of youth on Buffalo's West Side engages in a somewhat unusual activity for their age. They pack cans, label, and market salsa made from locally grown produce at local retail stores and markets. These young entrepreneurs are members of a youth business cooperative overseen by the Massachusetts Avenue Project (MAP), a nonprofit group working with youth to strengthen local and regional food systems in inner-city neighborhoods in Buffalo, New York. The youth business cooperative is a small component of Growing Green, a multifaceted program that empowers youth to improve food environments and transform their neighborhoods. In this case study, we describe the efforts of the Growing Green youth to revitalize their food environments and neighborhoods, and how planners and local governments can assist such efforts.

Context

MAP focuses its efforts predominantly on Buffalo's West Side.[11] The neighborhood has a diverse population that includes immigrants from many different countries. Despite its rich diversity, the neighborhood faces considerable challenges. Between 1990 and 2000, the area's population decreased from 11,403 to 9,146, a drop of 19.8 percent. Not surprisingly, vacancy rates are high: in 2000, the neighborhood had a housing vacancy rate of 22.3 percent, compared to 15.7 percent for the entire city. About 40 percent of the neighborhood's population lives in poverty, much higher than the city's 26.6 percent (UB 2003). Youth, in particular, face significant economic hardships: about 90 percent of the families living in poverty have children younger than 18 living with them.

The Problem

A comprehensive neighborhood food system plan of Buffalo's West Side documented significant food insecurity and limited access to affordable and nutritious food in the neighborhood. The *Food for Growth* authors found that "food items in the West Side were on average more costly" and that "food was found to be closer to expiration in stores on the West Side than the same food items found in chain stores" (UB 2003). The lack of affordable and nutritious food in the West Side neighborhood is exacerbated by the fact that roughly 50 percent of households there do not have access to a vehicle. Residents rely on public transit or other transportation arrangements to reach distant food stores that sell healthful and affordable food. One resident reported that a round trip to a food store took her about two hours on the bus, not including the time spent waiting for the bus at the stop or shopping (UB 2003).

The Solution

Under MAP's leadership, a partnership of organizations and individuals are implementing the recommendations of the *Food for Growth* plan by empowering West Side youth to improve their food environment and transform their neighborhood. With funding assistance from several entities, including the City of Buffalo's Summer Youth program and USDA's Community Food Project, MAP employs about 50 West Side youth through its flagship Growing Green program to increase access to food for West Side residents and, more broadly, to help revitalize their neighborhood.

Community gardening on vacant lots. Vacant lots are a familiar sight on Buffalo's West Side. According to *Food for Growth,* 22 percent of all land parcels on the West Side are vacant, higher than the 15 percent of parcel vacancy in the city. These parcels impose significant costs on the city government as a result of maintenance costs, liability insurance costs, and lost property taxes. The presence of these vacant lots also triggers disinvestment in adjacent properties, nudging entire city blocks into a downward spiral. There are less tangible costs as well. Residents associate vacant lots with drug and criminal activity, abandonment, and physical and social distress. Not far from parks that Olmsted designed to rejuvenate the city for residents, a new generation of gardeners work to transform these vacant parcels into green pockets in the neighborhood.

Each summer about 40 West Side youth, ages 11 to 18, tend raised bed gardens on 1,500 square feet of formerly abandoned vacant lots. Guided by the MAP staff, the youth use organic and sustainable methods to grow a variety of vegetables and flowers. The youth cook and consume as well as sell their crops, which include tomatoes, zucchinis, collards, herbs, and sunflowers, to name a few. The Growing Green gardens offer a safe and attractive gathering space for young and adult residents in a neighborhood, frequently challenged by drug and criminal activity. Lauren Breen (2007), the executive director of the Massachusetts Avenue Project, notes the importance of these green pockets for the neighborhood:

> These gardens represent hope for the neighborhood. They are a venue where people interact. They are an oasis in a distressed neighborhood. They attract people from the neighborhood and from outside the neighborhood.

Community gardens demonstrate that community-led transformation in disinvested neighborhoods is possible.

Youth business entrepreneurship. In addition to making physical improvements through gardens, Growing Green focuses on community economic development. Each year Growing Green offers income generation and job training to young people. About 40 youth work on Growing Green projects during the summer months, while another 10 continue to work throughout the school year. During the summer, the young people's salaries are paid by Buffalo's "Summer Youth Employment" program, a workforce development program for youth. During the school year, a smaller group of youth work as peer trainers at k-12 schools and after-school church programs, training other youth in healthy eating and food system issues. The monies for school-year salaries are partially recouped through program fees paid by client sites. The youth are paid about $7 per hour for their work.

In addition to making physical improvements through gardens, Growing Green focuses on community economic development. Each year Growing Green offers income generation and job training to young people.

Figure 4-38. Growing Green peer leaders at a school garden.

Angelika Breinlich

The latest venture of Growing Green youth is Growing Green Works, a youth-led cooperative food business that develops and markets value-added food products made from locally grown and organic produce. As part of the program, youth participate in a business development educational program. Now in its second year of operation, Growing Green Works has two signature products, a salsa (Super Duper Salsa) and a chili starter (Amazing Chili Starter) made from produce purchased from a local Community Supported Agriculture farm.

The Massachusetts Avenue Project

The Massachusetts Avenue Project

Figure 4-39. Growing Green (GG) entrepreneur and GG value-added products.

Youth are involved in all aspects of the business, including planning, marketing, and placement of the products, as well as learning and conducting financial analyses for their business. The youth use a combination of direct sales to consumers at area markets as well as sales through specialty food retailers to market their products. In 2006-07, Growing Green Works sold 820 jars of its chili starter and 93 jars of salsa. The sales generated $2,719 in revenues, which allowed the business to recover packaging costs as well as earn a modest profit of $300.[12] Growing Green Works products have been sold at 13 retail destinations, including local grocery stores and farmers markets. Plans are underway to introduce the products at other retail locations as well. As this business continues to scale up, Growing Green Works has the potential to offer modest employment opportunities to neighborhood youth. Growing Green Program Director, Diane Picard, hopes the program will eventually be able to generate enough revenue to pay the wages of all Growing Green youth (Picard, 2007).

Youth leadership. Participation in Growing Green encourages West Side youth to think critically about their food system and to play a leadership role in effecting change within their local food system through a vast array of activities. Since 2003, about 30 youth have been trained as peer educators. These peer trainers teach healthy eating and food systems workshops in area schools, after-school programs, and churches, and co-host youth conferences. Each year, as part of the "National Eat In, Act Out Week," the youth also host a community barbecue during which they cook for local residents and perform skits to highlight the importance of local and sustainable food systems. Through participation in Growing Green, youth report gaining useful leadership skills: a recent survey reported that 73 percent of the young people in the program say that participation in the program increased their leadership skills and their ability to set goals and make better decisions (Raja 2007).

Figure 4-40. *Growing Green peer leaders and MAP staff (in green t-shirts) conducting an after-school healthy eating workshop at the Bennett Park Montessori School.*

The Massachusetts Avenue Project

Young people working in Growing Green learn about healthy eating by cooking and consuming healthy meals made from the produce they grow during weekly community dinners to which all neighborhood residents are invited.

Promoting healthy eating behavior among youth. Young people working in Growing Green learn about healthy eating by cooking and consuming healthy meals made from the produce they grow during weekly community dinners to which all neighborhood residents are invited. Participation in this experiential program has a statistically measurable impact on their eating habits. For example, a survey found a statistically significant (p=0.07) drop in the number of days youth in the program consumed fast food per week before (2.25 days per week) and after (1.65 days per week) (Raja 2007).

To be sure, participation in Growing Green is a necessary but not sufficient strategy for promoting healthy eating among youth in this neighborhood. The same survey reports that even after learning about healthful foods and healthy eating, the young people's consumption of fruits and vegetables does not increase concomitantly. The explanation for this disconnect is complex. Youth may be unable to access fruits and vegetables at home and in their neighborhood. As one young person explained during an interview:

> I eat what my mom cooks. She doesn't go to Tops or Wegmans a lot. She goes to Aldi's. She doesn't like to take me grocery shopping anymore because I read the labels, and it annoys her. I like to eat vegetables…but I live in the hood. You know what I mean. Do you see any stores selling apples here? Sometimes I cook for myself. I make my own lunch sometimes. Sometimes I eat what I can get, like I go to this corner store and grab something.

In fact, in the neighborhood where this young man lives, there are no stores where he can purchase healthful foods. The family frequently shop at corner stores. The youth's mother occasionally shops at a large discount grocery store (Aldi's) and less frequently at Tops and Wegmans, which carry a relatively larger selection of healthful foods but where the prices are higher. The youth is often responsible for creating his meals. For this and other participants in the Growing Green program, the family's limited resources as well as a lack of access to healthful foods are barriers to eating healthful foods. Thus, efforts to remove barriers in the food environments—such as by facilitating community gardens and farmers markets in underserved neighborhoods or attracting affordable healthful food retail—are a critical link in facilitating healthy eating and overall public health.

How Did Youth-Led Transformation of West Side Neighborhoods Come About?

The youth-led transformation of the West Side is a product of numerous factors , including MAP's leadership and its commitment to the neighborhood; the availability of a comprehensive food assessment and plan that informs MAP's work; and the support, financial and otherwise, of a broad partnership of organizations (including the local government).

MAP's experience of working in the West Side neighborhood dates back to 1992 when a group of residents organized to construct a neighborhood playground on Massachusetts Avenue, a street that lacked any amenities for area youth. Since then, MAP has continued to evolve in its mission, responding to the needs of the neighborhood. MAP's mission is to "[nurture] the growth of a diverse and equitable community food system to promote local economic opportunities, access to affordable, nutritious food, and social-change education." Through their work in the neighborhood, MAP staff has earned the trust of residents, especially its younger residents for whom MAP staff have become mentors and role models.

In addition to its efforts to build ties with the community, MAP's work is guided by significant planning efforts. In 2003, Growing Green commissioned the Department of Urban and Regional Planning at the University at Buffalo to prepare a comprehensive food assessment and plan to strengthen the food system on in the West Side neighborhood. The plan, *Food for Growth,* outlines four strategies to guide MAP's work:

Enhancing local food production through land use planning. To pursue this strategy, the plan recommends increasing food production on available vacant lots within the city; the plan recommends that the city recognize urban agriculture as a permissible land use deserving of the city's protection and investment

Promoting food-based economic development. The plan reports that the food sector on Buffalo's West Side contributes an astounding $42.9 million to the county's economy. The plan recommends that MAP expand its microenterprise program to offer small loans to food entrepreneurs on the West Side.

Increasing transportation access to food. The plan notes that West Side residents have limited transportation access to food. It recommends that MAP work with the Niagara Frontier Transportation Authority to improve public transit options for residents.

Promoting youth-based economic development through food projects. The plan notes that MAP has considerable experience in working with youth. The plan recommends that MAP educate children about growing, preparing, and eating healthy food, and train them as food entrepreneurs.

The *Food for Growth* plan, which received numerous planning awards, including the 2004 American Institute of Certified Planners (AICP) award, helped MAP leverage nearly a quarter-million dollars in funding through a Community Food Project grant of the United States Department of Agriculture (USDA) to implement the recommendations from *Food for Growth*. MAP has also received grants and financial assistance through a number of other government agencies and private foundations, , including the City of Buffalo's Summer Youth Workforce Development program, the Robert Wood Johnson Foundation's Healthy Eating by Design Program, and the Oshei Foundation, to name a few.

In addition to engaging in on-the-ground food planning, MAP has begun to build its organizational capacity. Under the leadership of its executive director, Lauren Breen, MAP is engaging in an extensive strategic planning process for the organization, which includes streamlining its programs and identifying resources required to support these programs.

Lessons for Planners

The work of grassroots organizations, such as MAP, in transforming local food systems can be supported by planners in a number of different ways.

Facilitate land acquisition and permanent land tenure for community gardens. Acquisition of land and lack of permanency in land ownership is one of the principal barriers to initiating and sustaining community gardens even when vacant land is abundant in a municipality.

Consider the example of Buffalo. Growing Green operates 57 garden beds on seven former vacant lots covering about 1,500 square feet. MAP owns two of the lots (purchased at a city auction), four belong to the city, and one belongs to a private individual who allows MAP to garden on it. To gain access to city-owned lots, Growing Green relies on Grassroots Gardens, another nonprofit, whose mission is "to help people create and sustain community gardens on city-owned vacant properties throughout Buffalo." Grassroots Gardens facilitates lease transactions for community gardens with the city and provides liability insurance for all community gardens in Buffalo (Grassroots website). Facilitated by Grassroots Gardens, MAP has a five-year lease arrangement with the city (November 2005 to December 2010) for the use of city-owned lots for gardening. However, the lease can be broken by the city with a 30-day written notice. The short-term duration and the fragility of the lease arrangement threaten the long-term stability of community gardens in Buffalo. According to Diane Picard, the program direct of Growing Green, the city considers community gardens as a temporary use of the land that may be subject to removal in the face of a development project.

Acquisition of land and lack of permanency in land ownership is one of the principal barriers to initiating and sustaining community gardens even when vacant land is abundant in a municipality.

Picard points to examples of land protection in other communities as possible solutions to these threats of development. For instance, the city could engage in a 99-year lease and relax the condition that the lease can be broken with a 30-day written notice. A land trust could be established to protect existing gardens from being developed into something else in the future. The city could also transfer the ownership of community garden lots to community organizations. Such an action by the city would symbolically demonstrate the importance of community gardens as a valuable public good.

Information generation. Based on her experience, Picard suggests that the first step in making headway on food security and healthy eating in any community is by making city officials aware about the enormity of the problem of lack of healthful food access in cities like Buffalo. She notes that planners have a role to play in this process by studying and documenting the incidence of food insecurity and recommending policies that ensure food security. Planners can also play a role by using regulatory tools, such as zoning, to dedicate space to community gardens and food-related activities. Picard concedes that getting planners attention is not an easy task since the problem of food security is fairly new to planning and not as easily visible as, say, vacant or derelict housing.

Facilitate site suitability analysis for community gardens. Richard Tobe, the Economic Development Commissioner for Buffalo, also sees community gardens, whether for vegetables or flowers, as very valuable for an urban environment in that they improve the land and "hold it for future use." When asked about the role of planners in supporting community gardens, the commissioner suggests that planners can lend their services to communities during the initial stages of locating and developing appropriate sites for a community garden. In addition, in case these sites are located on contaminated brownfields, planners can help educate communities about how to best mitigate the effects of contamination.

Tobe also recommends that planners pay attention to reconnecting the rural farm operations to the urban core in a region, a perspective greatly supported by community food advocates and planners. He notes, for example, the city of Buffalo is only 41 square miles, whereas Erie County, the city's host county, covers 1,200 square miles with a large number of family farms. Instead of reinventing agriculture, he believes that efforts should be undertaken to encourage local retail, institutions, and restaurants to buy locally grown goods and services.

Nurture and support community partnerships on food. Like the work of community organizations nationwide, MAP's work in the West Side neighborhood is made possible in part by its willingness to collaborate in a number of partnerships with a wide variety of individuals and organizations. MAP's partners include local universities (e.g., the University at Buffalo Schools of Law, Architecture and Planning, and Public Health and Health Professions), local schools and school district (e.g., Bennett Park Montessori public school), local farms (e.g., Native Offerings Community Supported Agricultural Farm), and other local nonprofit organizations (e.g., the Buffalo Niagara Medical Campus). Establishing and sustaining these partnerships increases MAP's ability to engage in complex work that demands a diverse set of skills and significant resources otherwise difficult to provide through a single organization.

The efforts in Buffalo to build healthy food environments within "food deserts" demonstrate the important role of youth and grassroots planning in creating change. Ensuring long-term food security and access to healthful foods will depend on elected officials, urban planners, and citizens' full participation in these grassroots efforts.

CHAPTER 5

Understanding and Measuring
Food Environments

No matter whether they play a direct or indirect role in improving food environments in their communities, it is important for planners to understand that food environments are complex and ever-changing. Below we offer some characteristics that will help planners frame and understand food environments in their communities. Following this, we outline indicators that planners can use to measure the condition of food environments. These characteristics and indicators are by no means exhaustive and are not the only way to frame a food environment; we offer them as a starting point for practitioners interested in understanding their community's food environment.

CHARACTERISTICS OF FOOD ENVIRONMENTS

The Food Environment Includes a Variety of Food Destinations

A number of popular and academic reports (e.g., Morland et al. 2006 and 2002) point to the absence of conventional supermarkets as indicative of an unhealthful food environment, citing evidence that supermarkets carry more healthful produce as compared to small grocery stores and convenience stores. However, people obtain food from a much wider array of venues. These include where people:

- buy food through conventional retail (e.g., supermarkets, grocery stores, and convenience stores) and direct producer-to-consumer marketing retail (e.g., community-supported agriculture, market basket programs, rural and urban farm stands, and farmers' markets);

- grow their own food (in their backyards or on community gardens);

- obtain it through membership in institutions (school cafeterias; farm-to-school programs); or

- receive it through emergency providers (e.g., food banks and food pantries) during times of economic distress.

In short, food environments include a large variety of food destinations where people can obtain healthful foods to eat. In areas underserved by supermarkets, alternative food venues—such as farmers' markets, community gardens, market basket programs, small bodegas, farm-to-school programs, etc.—are increasingly playing a greater role in promoting access to healthful foods. For example, in Buffalo, New York, more than 50 community gardens are used to grow food. While it is unlikely that food grown in community gardens can become the primary source of food for urban households, it can certainly supplement their access to fresh produce.

In summary, planners need to recognize that people can obtain healthful foods from a variety of food destinations. It is important for planners to understand what types of food destinations are available, if any, in people's neighborhoods; whether they sell healthful foods; and then determine how planners can assist in increasing access to healthful foods.

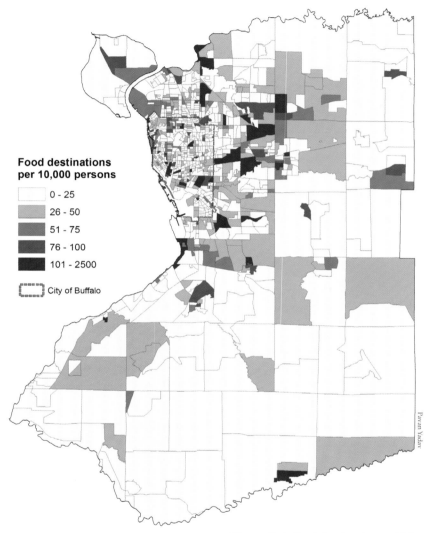

Food destinations per 10,000 persons

- 0 - 25
- 26 - 50
- 51 - 75
- 76 - 100
- 101 - 2500

⌐ ⌐ City of Buffalo

Pavan Yadav

Figure 5-1. *Food destinations within Erie County, New York.*

Spatial Disparities in the Food Environment

Understanding the spatial configuration of food destinations within a community—their location, proximity, distribution, and density—can inform planners and policy makers about the disparities in food environments. Are supermarkets clustered in certain types of neighborhoods? Are fast-food restaurants concentrated in low-income neighborhoods? Do convenience stores cluster around schools? Answers to these questions will shed light on disparities in the food environment.

Although researchers have done only limited work on the spatial distribution of food destinations, some data have begun to emerge. A study by Raja et al. (2008) of Erie County, New York, showed that among the more common types of retail food destinations (supermarkets, small grocery stores, convenience stores, and restaurants), restaurants are the most equitably spread across the county's neighborhoods (census block groups), while supermarkets are clustered within a few block groups of the county (Figure 5-1). This clustering also has a racial dimension: the study authors found that, on average, predominantly black neighborhoods in Erie County have 0.43 times the number of supermarkets within a five-minute walking distance when compared to predominantly white neighborhoods (Figure 5-2). Shortcomings and disparities in the food environment also have implications for public health outcomes, such as obesity (Morland et al. 2006) and diabetes (Mari Gallaghar Consulting and Research Group 2006). Planners can use their spatial and GIS skills to document the spatial configuration and disparities of the food environment in their communities and thereby contribute to the interdisciplinary efforts to facilitate healthy eating.

Quality of Food at Existing Food Destinations

Knowing the spatial distribution of food destinations is clearly not a sufficient indicator for judging the quality of the food environment. In addition to knowing where and how food destinations are distributed within a community, it is

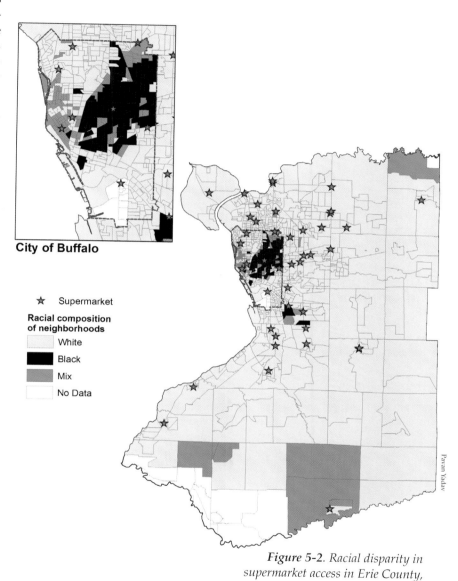

City of Buffalo

★ Supermarket

Racial composition of neighborhoods

- White
- Black
- Mix
- No Data

Pavan Yadav

Figure 5-2. Racial disparity in supermarket access in Erie County, New York.

In addition to understanding whether available food destinations sell nutritious meals, it is important to understand whether the available food is affordable, and whether it meets the cultural preferences of residents.

important for planners to understand the quality of food available at these destinations. A number of existing studies (Moore and Diez Roux 2006; Morland et al. 2006 and 2001; Zenk et al. 2005) on the limitations of food environments use the absence of a conventional supermarket as an indicator of the unavailability of healthful food in a community, citing evidence (Sallis et al. 1986) that conventional supermarkets carry fresher produce and a greater variety of food products than other food destinations, such as smaller grocery stores and convenience stores. While this may be true in some instances, planners would do well to carefully examine the quality of foods available in food destinations within their particular communities.

According to the Community Food Security Coalition (CFSC), a community cannot be considered food secure unless the food environment provides nutritionally adequate, affordable, and culturally appropriate food. The topic of nutritional adequacy is complex and falls more within the purview of public health and nutrition professionals. Thus, planners interested in improving food environments have to partner with the public health professionals in their community.

Nonetheless, it is important for planners to have a basic understanding of the quality of food at available destinations. One way to do so is to judge whether an existing food environment allows residents to assemble an affordable nutritious meal according to the U.S. Department of Agriculture's (USDA) meal plans. In particular, USDA's Thrifty Food Plan (TFP) is a good place for planners to start with since it is used by the federal government to determine the maximum food stamp entitlement for eligible recipients (www.cnpp.usda.gov/Publications/FoodPlans/MiscPubs/TFP2006Report. pdf). The plan outlines the minimum nutritional requirements by demographic group. USDA also publishes data on the cost for purchasing food according to the TFP guidelines. The TFP guidelines may be used to develop a survey of food venues to discern whether people can indeed obtain affordable nutritious meals within their communities.

In addition to understanding whether available food destinations sell nutritious meals, it is important to understand whether the available food is affordable, and whether it meets the cultural preferences of residents. Short et al.'s (2007) study of three ethnic neighborhoods in San Francisco offers a good example of how planners can assess a food environment. Using a combination of USDA's nutrition guidelines and CFSC's expansive definition of quality, the authors found that small grocery stores carried nutritious, affordable, and culturally appropriate foods for the mostly immigrant residents, challenging previous reports of poor quality food in small stores.

The Food Environment Is Interlinked with Other Environments.
The food environment does not exist in a vacuum. It is integrated with the built, social, economic, and cultural environments of a community. Indeed, an identical food environment in two neighborhoods with different social/economic environments can result in disparate eating experiences and health outcomes for residents of the two neighborhoods. For example, in a high-income neighborhood, the absence of a grocery store is not as great a limitation when compared to a low-income neighborhood where automobile ownership rates are low. In other words, residents in higher-income neighborhoods most likely have a greater capacity to overcome the barriers imposed by their food environment.

Food Environments Are Shaped by People
Food environments are shaped by the people within them. For example, convenience stores, typically known for stocking limited healthy food options, have been known to respond to customers' demands by, for example, stocking ethnic

foods in immigrant neighborhoods (UB 2003). Likewise, in many food desert communities, residents have transformed vacant lots into thriving urban gardens that supply fresh, nutritious produce. People within the food environment are not inert consumers; they are food citizens—foodizens—whose capabilities, resources, and values shape their eating experience within the food environment as well as the surrounding food environment. By focusing simply on the supply side of the food access problem, such as the absence of supermarkets, we run the risk of overlooking the possibility of residents as agents of change and ignore the importance of demand in shaping the food environment.

The Food Environment Can Be Measured at Many Scales

For planning purposes, we can distinguish the food environment on at least three scales. The first is a regional food environment, which encompasses multimunicipal or multicounty areas. The regional food environment can be coterminus with a foodshed (Kloppenburg et al. 1996), an area that produces and supplies food in an environmentally sustainable manner to the people living within the regional food environment. In theory, a regional food environment may be able to produce enough food for residents living within the region. A regional food environment may support a community supported agriculture program, linking cities with rural farms. The municipal food environment includes food destinations that residents can access within a city, town, or a village at places of residence, work, play/school, and along routes connecting these. These include large farmers' markets (e.g., the Dane County farmers' market in Madison, Wisconsin), large supermarkets, and food shopping districts. The municipal food environment in an urban area is likely to have less food production capacity than, say, a regional food environment but nonetheless may include food production sites such as urban farms and community gardens. Finally, the neighborhood food environment refers to the food environment available to residents within the immediacy of their neighborhoods, such as within walking, bicycling, and short driving distances, where they can obtain food. While every neighborhood food environment may not have access to a large farmers' market, it would be beneficial for residents to access grocery stores or smaller neighborhood markets (e.g., the neighborhood markets in Kichener, Ontario).

Distinguishing between the three scales is important for a number of reasons. First, access to food is inherently an issue of scale. For example, a resident living in a city with abundant farmers' markets may still live in a neighborhood without a grocery store. A city-scale analysis of the problem would simply overlook this problem on the neighborhood scale. The second, related reason is that the solutions for promoting food security are scale specific as well. In the previous example, a neighborhood-scale analysis of the situation would recommend, say, the creation of effective mass transit to facilitate a neighborhood's access to the city's farmers' markets. A city-scale problem, if there were one, would require a different strategy. Finally, basic market considerations suggest that not all types of food destinations can be sustained at all scales. For instance, it may not be feasible to have a large farmers' market at each street corner, while it may be feasible to have a small grocery store in each neighborhood. Thus, the articulation, analyses, and solutions necessary for planning a healthy food environment requires that planners recognize the multi-scalar nature of the food environment.

MEASURING ACCESS TO HEALTHFUL FOODS

Several measurable indicators can help planners understand the problems and opportunities within a community's food environment. These indicators can be classified into three categories: food environment indicators; public infrastructure indicators; and demographic indicators.

People within the food environment are not inert consumers; they are food citizens—foodizens—whose capabilities, resources, and values shape their eating experience within the food environment as well as the surrounding food environment.

Food Environment Indicators

Planners can document the availability of different types of food retail destinations for community residents.

- Farmers markets
- Grocery stores
- Supermarkets
- Bodegas and other ethnic specialty markets
- Restaurants
- Community supported agriculture drop-off sites
- Farm stands
- Food banks and pantries (emergency food source)

Then, planners can document the availability of food production destinations for community residents.

- Farms (Rural and urban; conventional, organic, family farms, CSAs; etc.)
- Community gardens

Finally, they can document the quality of food available at these food destinations.

- Nutritional quality
- Affordability
- Cultural appropriateness

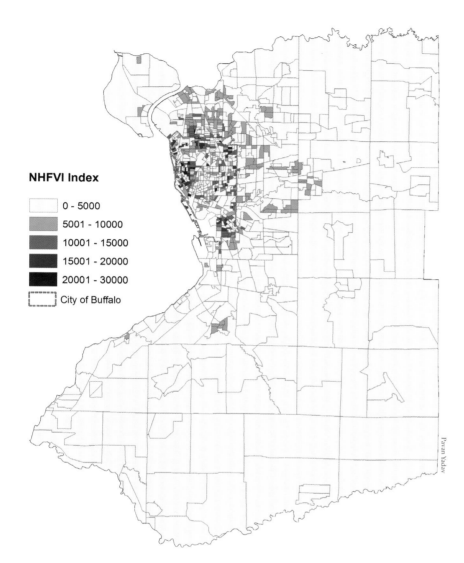

NHFVI Index

- 0 - 5000
- 5001 - 10000
- 10001 - 15000
- 15001 - 20000
- 20001 - 30000
- City of Buffalo

Pavan Yadav

Figure 5-3. Relative access to healthful versus unhealthful foods in Erie County, New York. [This map shows the relative imbalance in access to healthful versus unhealthful foods in Erie County using a Neighborhood Healthful Foods Vulnerability Index (NHFVI). Darker areas represent more vulnerable neighborhoods (block groups). In these neighborhoods, residents' access to the number of healthful stores (e.g., supermarkets, green grocers, and farmers' markets) is proportionately lower than their exposure to unhealthful food destinations (e.g., convenience stores and fast-food restaurants selling processed foods). The index is adjusted by the size of the population in each block group.]

In documenting the food environment indicators, planners must pay particular attention to relative access to healthful versus unhealthful foods. In any particular neighborhood, the proliferation of stores that sell only unhealthful snacks is less of a concern if the neighborhood is also fortunate enough to have a grocery store that provides residents with access to fresh fruits and vegetables. Figure 5-3 maps this relative access in Erie County, New York using Geographic Information Systems. Such maps can help planners and public health experts identify areas that require particular attention and assistance from policy makers.

Public Infrastructure and Built Environment Indicators

Planners need to ask themselves two important questions:

- Does public transit take into account access to food destinations, especially for connecting neighborhoods with low auto-ownership rates?

- Does mixed-use development include provisions for healthful food retail?

The absence of grocery stores and other healthful food destinations is problematic in neighborhoods with low auto ownership rates, especially when these neighborhoods are poorly connected to food destinations via public transit. The quality of these connections—the schedules of the buses, the routes, the number of transfers, wait time, etc.—are particularly important in judging access to healthful food destinations. In Erie County, New York, major supermarkets appear to be well-connected by bus lines (see figure 5-4), but a trip chain analysis and focus groups with residents revealed that in poorer neighborhoods (e.g., the West Side of Buffalo, New York) residents report spending about two hours to complete a grocery trip, not including the time waiting at the bus stop or the time spent during grocery shopping (UB 2003).

Vulnerability and Disparity Indicators

As reported elsewhere in this report, lower-income and minority neighborhoods have lower access to supermarkets and other healthful food destinations. Therefore, it is important to examine how the food environment affects different groups of people. Are food destinations accessible to people of varying incomes, age, ethnic backgrounds? Planners might use the following factors to map access to healthful food:

- Income
- Age
- Ethnicity/Race
- Auto ownership

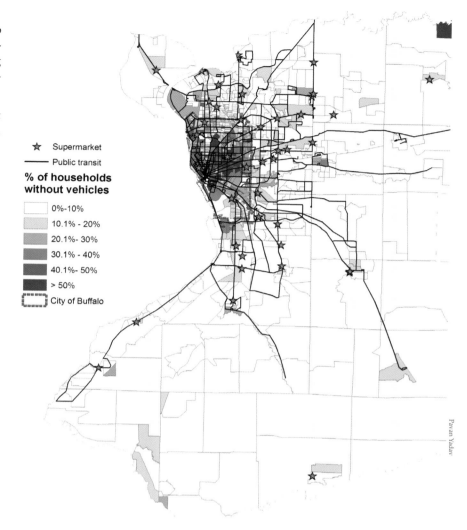

Figure 5-4. Supermarket access via public transit in Erie County, New York.

Figure 5-2 (above) shows the distribution of supermarkets by racial com-position of neighborhoods in Erie County, New York. Predominantly black neighborhoods (with > 60 percent of households identifying themselves as black) have very few supermarkets.

CHAPTER 6

Planning Strategies
to Improve Food Environments
and Facilitate Healthy Eating

As the case studies in this PAS Report have demonstrated, planners can contribute to improving food environments using a variety of strategies. Some involve removal of regulatory barriers, while others are more active strategies, such as dedicating land to community gardens. While the strategies used by a particular community are likely to be context-specific, we believe that the following five broad strategies can be helpful in promoting access to healthful foods:

1. Information generation
2. Program implementation
3. Facilitation and coordination
4. Plan making and design
5. Zoning and regulatory reform

Indeed, in nearly all the case studies presented in this report, the healthy eating efforts of each community were girded by extensive community food assessments that identified the strengths and weaknesses in their food systems and food environments.

INFORMATION GENERATION

Planners have long played the role of information generators within their communities. Kaufman (2004) extends describes four areas in which planners can play this role in strengthening food systems. They can:

- assess the community's food system by conducting community food assessments;

- illuminate market gaps showing documenting how the conventional food system fails to meet demand for food;

- provide measured, empirical evidence on the benefits of the community food system; and

- document more clearly the external costs of the conventional food system.

While all four areas are important to strengthen community food systems, the first two—conducting community food assessments and documenting how the conventional food system fails to meet the demand for foods—are especially important for facilitating healthy eating in a community. Indeed, in nearly all the case studies presented in this report, the healthy eating efforts of each community were girded by extensive community food assessments that identified the strengths and weaknesses in their food systems and food environments.

What are community food assessments, and how can planners go about conducting them? Pothukuchi (2004) describes community food assessments as a "novel manifestation" of community assessments that involve "activities to systematically collect and disseminate information on selected community characteristics so that community leaders and agencies may devise appropriate strategies to improve their localities." Such processes have been applied by planners to a variety of issues ranging from transportation to economic development. When applied to the notion of food, a community food assessment is described as:

> a collaborative and participatory process that systematically examines a broad range of community food issues and assets, so as to inform change actions to make the community more food secure. (www.worldhungeryear.com)

The process of generating information through an assessment can inform policy makers about the availability of food resources in a community, the food-related concerns of community members, as well as potential solutions for addressing these concerns (Pothukuchi et al. 2002). Assessments can serve as an integral component of a broader community and regional planning and policy-making effort to promote healthful foods.

COORDINATION AND FACILITATION

Planners often play the role of facilitators, coordinators, and negotiators in the land development process, and they can contribute greatly to building healthy cities by extending this role to the area of improving food environments. The three areas of facilitation and coordination for planners are described in the next three subsections.

Coordination Between Local Government Agencies and Departments

Food-related issues do not neatly fall into the purview of any single local government agency or department. With their interdisciplinary skills, planners can coordinate between relevant agencies and departments, such as the local public health agency, public works, engineering, inspections, etc., to ensure that planning recommendations related to food do not fall through the proverbial cracks of the local government bureaucracy. In this role, planners can also facilitate and coordinate the efforts to create and support a food policy council. Of course, food planners can also make a significant contribution by bringing food to the attention of planners working within traditional areas of planning. A few examples follow:

- Transportation: Transit routes can be designed to facilitate access to supermarkets, farmers' markets, and other healthful food destinations.
- Environment: Plans for creating and protecting green space can include community gardens.
- Economic development: Community supported agriculture programs that bring healthy local produce to urban consumers are smart economic development and smart food planning, and therefore merit the attention of economic development planners.

Coordination Between Stakeholders of a Food System

A commonly cited barrier for a well-functioning food system is the lack of connection between its producers, processors, and consumers. For example, the absence of fruits and vegetables in a community, even when they are available in plentiful at regional farms, may be attributed to a broken food system that fails to connect local growers with consumers. Planners can play a significant role by connecting various actors in a food system. This has the potential of increasing healthful foods in communities, as well as regenerating the local food economy. The various actors in the food system that planners can work to reconnect are:

A commonly cited barrier for a well-functioning food system is the lack of connection between its producers, processors, and consumers

- rural farmers and urban school districts (e.g, through farm-to-school programs);
- farmers and consumers (e.g., through farmers' markets); and
- local food producers and local food processors (e.g., by spearheading buy local campaigns).

PROGRAMMATIC EFFORTS

Planners can also act as primary actors in strengthening community food systems and promoting healthy eating. Below we provide some examples of this.

Supermarket and Grocery Store Development

Planners can actively engage supermarket retailers to develop stores in underserved urban and rural neighborhoods. A number of steps may help this process.

- Facilitate the assembly of land for medium to large supermarkets in urban areas where land parcels are small and typically not available in a contiguous fashion. In rural areas, this would be less of a concern.
- Fast-track development approval for supermarket retailers in urban and rural municipalities.
- Explore the use of economic development incentives to attract supermarkets in urban and rural areas.
- Encourage mixed-use neighborhood design and redevelopment to include small and midsize grocery stores (e.g., 3,000 to 20,000 square feet) (APA Food Policy Guide, #3A).

Healthy Corner Grocery Stores

A critique of small grocery stores and convenience stores is that they carry a limited amount of healthful foods compared to supermarkets. However, these stores constitute a significant proportion of food destinations available

Planners can make creative use of economic development funds to help small stores make capital investments that allow the purchase of refrigeration equipment to store fresh fruits and vegetables, or to scale up their inventory and staff.

in low-income and minority neighborhoods (Raja et al. 2008). Perhaps even more important than attracting supermarkets in these neighborhoods is the need to assist small to medium grocery stores in carrying more healthful foods. Rather than chasing supermarkets that are likely to put small food stores out of business, planners should find creative ways to support the transformation of small grocery stores into healthy food venues (Raja et al. 2008) or to support the establishment of new small to medium grocery stores.

Small to medium grocery stores also have the additional appeal that they fit into the built environment fabric of urban neighborhoods and other compact neighborhoods in terms of square footage requirements as well as aesthetic appeal.

Planners can make creative use of economic development funds to help small stores make capital investments that allow the purchase of refrigeration equipment to store fresh fruits and vegetables, or to scale up their inventory and staff. (See the Philadelphia case study in Chapter 4 for an excellent model.)

Farmers' Markets

Planners can support the creation and sustenance of farmers markets in a number of ways:

- Planners can conduct site suitability analysis and market studies to identify prime location for farmers' markets.

- They can recruit regional farmers and offer other logistical support for creating and sustaining farmers' markets in their communities.

- Urban designers can develop design guidelines suitable for farmers' markets.

- Planners can work with public works officials to facilitate the markets' access to public electricity and water supply.

Community Gardens, Edible Landscapes, and Urban Farms

While planning departments probably lack the expertise to run and manage a community garden per se, they certainly have the skills to facilitate a community gardening program whereby the planning department identifies suitable lands for gardening and coordinates their allocation to interested individuals and organizations.

On publicly owned lands, such as schoolyards, parks, greenways, and tax-foreclosed properties, planners can support the development of vegetable gardens, edible landscaping, and related infrastructure, and the formation of partnerships with community-based nonprofits serving low-income residents for garden-related programs (APA Policy #3A).

Institutional Purchasing

Finally, planners can create or support programs to encourage institutional purchasing of healthful foods. For example, cafeterias that prepare and sell food within schools, prisons, hospitals, universities, and even local government offices can be required to offer locally grown healthful foods to their customers.

PLAN MAKING AND DESIGN

We outline below ways in which food environments may be improved through the use of traditional and some nontraditional planning tools.

Stand-Alone Food Plans

Planners can modify the generic planning process to prepare a stand-alone food system plan for their community. Such a plan can focus on one aspect of the food system, such as planning for access to healthful foods, or it can be a comprehensive food plan that examines several aspects of a food system, such as production, processing, distribution, consumption, and disposal of food. A community's food plan should be based on a thorough community food assessment to understand the strengths and weaknesses of the existing food system in a community. See Pothukuchi (2004 and 2002) for additional information on community food assessments. Below we outline the general steps that a municipality may follow for a planning process designed to prepare a stand-alone plan that promotes access to healthful foods for its residents. These steps may encompass some of the activities conducted as part of community food assessments.

Planning for healthful food environments requires a diverse set of skills, interdisciplinary knowledge, and varied experiences; as such, planners would do well to engage other relevant partners and stakeholders in guiding the planning process.

Phase I: Identify partners to participate in the planning process. Planning for healthful food environments requires a diverse set of skills, interdisciplinary knowledge, and varied experiences; as such, planners would do well to engage other relevant partners and stakeholders in guiding the planning process. Planners can draw upon individuals and organizations from different backgrounds to convene an advisory group to guide the community food planning process. These individuals and organizations include:

- advisory groups, such as Food Policy Councils;

- other departments within a local government, especially the local public health agency; and

- community food advocacy groups, local universities, and other organizations and individuals who have the experience and knowledge about local food systems.

Phase II: Devise a planning approach that fits the community's need. In consultation with planning partners, the lead planning agency can develop a planning approach and methodology to guide the planning process. This will involve deciding what phases III through VI might look like for a particular community.

Phase III: Visioning process. Like all planning processes, it is important to engage the community in a visioning exercise to articulate a community's values, ideals, and preferences for a healthy food environment. The visioning process must include diverse constituents, including:

- residents;

- food retailers;

- farmers;

- community gardeners; and

- food manufacturers and processors.

A successful and well-conducted visioning process will help planners articulate the goals and objectives of a community's healthful food environment plan.

Phase IV: Gather and analyze relevant data. Having established the goals and objectives of the plan, planners can gather relevant data to help them understand the state of the food environment in their municipality. Data for this plan can come from a variety of sources. Planners can use quantitative and GIS-based indicators described in Chapter 5 of this PAS Report to:

- document what types of food destinations are available to residents in a community;

- determine whether healthful food destinations are "redlining" particular neighborhoods; and

- determine whether particular population subgroups are especially vulnerable to the lack of healthful food sources.

Planners can also conduct focus groups and surveys with residents to document people's concerns regarding their food environment. Completion of this phase will illuminate the shortcomings and opportunities within a community's food environment.

We believe, however, that with a little creativity municipalities can undertake many improvements to their food environment with little impact on their budget.

Phase IV: Prepare preliminary recommendations and establish benchmarks for measuring progress. In this phase, planners can develop recommendations for improving access to healthful foods based on the preferences of community stakeholders as well as on the basis of precedents from other communities. Recommendations will vary widely, depending on the needs of a particular community. Some communities may find it important to protect lands for food production (in urban and rural areas); some may find it important to ensure availability of food retail in neighborhoods where rates of auto-ownership are low; and others may recommend changes in the municipal ordinance to limit unhealthful foods. Each recommendation must be accompanied by clear benchmarks to gauge progress after implementation of the plan. The plan must also make clear which agency will implement the recommendations, and what the likely fiscal impact of the recommendations will be on the municipal budget. (See the Marin County, California, plan highlighted in Chapter 4 for an example).

Phase V: Review findings and recommendations with interested stakeholders. Just as it is important to begin the planning process with a visioning session with community stakeholders, it is critical to receive feedback from them throughout the planning process.

Phase VI: Implement the recommendations and measure progress. Preparing for the implementation phase is critical for the success of any plan. The implementation of a plan to improve food environments is likely to face a number of implementation challenges that are important to anticipate. First, municipalities are often trapped by the need for resources. Adding food and healthy eating to their mix of responsibilities may be a daunting proposition. We believe, however, that with a little creativity municipalities can undertake many improvements to their food environment with little impact on their budget. Municipalities can partner with local colleges and universities to conduct food system research and develop baseline data and measure progress. They can create public-private partnerships to leverage funding, or pursue federal and state support, or a combination of all three. For example, a municipality could develop a public-private partnership wherein the municipality identifies suitable lots for community gardens for a community organization, which in turn makes these available to interested residents using agreed-upon terms. Having such a program will minimize maintenance costs of vacant lots for the municipality and increase access to fresh produce for residents.

Municipalities can also use public-private partnerships to leverage external funding for improving the food environment. For example, private nonprofit organizations are eligible to apply for the USDA Community Food Projects program that provides a one-time infusion of funds to help communities develop projects that tackle food insecurity as long as the organization can provide matching funds (www.csrees.usda.gov/fo/communityfoodprojects.cfm). Municipalities could set up a program whereby they offer matching funds to community groups whose proposals meet the objectives of the municipal healthy food environment plan. In addition to the federal government, a number of philanthropic foundations offer grant programs to improve food environments as well. For example, at least two of the communities (Louisville, Kentucky and Buffalo, New York) documented in Chapter 4 of this PAS Report received grant support from The Robert Wood Johnson Foundation.

Implementation of a food plan is also challenging because food does not fall within the purview of any single department in a local government. Thus, it is critical that planners work closely with other local government agencies, such the local public health agency, to identify clearly the entity responsible for implementing the recommendations food plan.

Finally, as part of the implementation process, it is critical to establish a timeline for implementing the various recommendations as well as clear benchmarks for the implementation phase. The Marin Countywide plan described in Chapter 4 is a good example of how recommendations may be associated with benchmarks, time horizons, and funding implications for the local government.

Inclusion of "Food" as an Element in Plans

Instead of a full-scale food planning process as described above, planners can also begin by incorporating food as an element in other plans, including comprehensive plans, transportation plans, and environmental plans, to name a few. As noted above in this report, food is currently included in comprehensive plans of several communities, including Marin County, California; Madison, Wisconsin; and Toronto, Ontario. This planning process can be similar to, although narrower in scope than, the process described for a stand-alone food plan in the previous section.

Designing with an Eye on Food

The following bulleted lists offer planners some ideas about how urban design, neighborhood, and area plans can better address the issue of making access to healthful food easier (and more attractive).

Food destinations and foodscapes as a design element.

- Develop plans and design guidelines that recognize the role of food destinations, such as farmers' markets, as potential center-pieces and icons of neighborhoods.

- Develop design guidelines that showcase the aesthetic quality of edible landscapes (i.e., "foodscapes").

Neighborhoods.

- Develop plans that include food destinations within a short distance of residential neighborhoods.

- Encourage mixed-use neighborhood design and redevelopment to include small and midsize grocery stores (e.g., 3,000 to 20,000 square feet), seasonal farmers markets, community-based and government nutrition programs, and open space and related infrastructure for community vegetable gardens to allow residents to grow their own food (APA Food Policy Guide, #3A).

- Develop neighborhood parks that feature edible plantings, community gardens, and youth gardens.

Connections.

- Develop area plans and design schemes in ways that encourage safe and convenient pedestrian, bike, transit connections between neighborhoods and the food sources described above (APA Food Policy Guide, #3A).

Instead of a full-scale food planning process as described above, planners can also begin by incorporating food as an element in other plans, including comprehensive plans, transportation plans, and environmental plans, to name a few.

*Examining and reforming
regulations, such as zoning
ordinances, to ensure they do not
impede the creation of a healthy
food environment is a good place
to start.*

- Support transit programs that improve connections between low-mobility neighborhoods on the one hand, and supermarkets, community gardens, food assistance programs (e.g., food pantries and soup kitchens), and health and social service providers on the other, with a view to reducing travel time and enhancing safe and convenient use (APA Food Policy Guide, #3A).

- Develop plans for locating healthful food sources, especially small markets and produce vendors, along transportation corridors and at nodes, such as transit stations. These corridors and nodes experience a high degree of foot traffic.

- Use edible landscaping alongside sidewalks and other pedestrian pathways.

REGULATORY AND ZONING REFORM

Planners can contribute greatly to promote healthy eating within their communities by removing barriers to the development of healthy food systems. Examining and reforming regulations, such as zoning ordinances, to ensure they do not impede the creation of a healthy food environment is a good place to start. Zoning codes regulate land uses (e.g., the establishment of food stores and vendors; establishing urban farms; etc.) in a municipality. It is important to critically examine existing zoning codes and licensing regulations to determine if they create barriers for creating a healthful food environment in a community. There are essentially two strategies in which zoning codes and licensing regulations may be used to shape the food environment:

1. To remove barriers, if any, to the establishment of a healthful food environment.

2. To limit the establishment of unhealthful food destinations within a community.

Clearly a combination of both strategies is likely to be a more effective mechanism for improving food environments; however, employing both strategies is not always feasible and trying to employ both may be more difficult than employing only one. We discuss each in turn and leave it to planners to judge what strategy is most relevant of their community.

First, zoning codes have the potential to create a barrier in establishing a healthful food environment. For example, zoning codes may prohibit the establishment of produce markets or produce stands in residential neighborhoods or outside a limited designated area. Such regulations create a barrier for vendors (or farmers) interested in selling produce, as well as for residents interested in purchasing the produce. This was certainly the case in Kitchener, Ontario, as described in Chapter 2 of this PAS Report. Fortunately, in Kitchener's case, the city deemed the neighborhood market to be in the public interest and ruled the market to be permissible. Nonetheless, the application process—to seek an exception to the city ordinance in order to set up the neighborhood market—imposed a considerable burden (in terms of time and human resources) on the partnership, which was facilitating the application for the neighborhood markets. Moreover, the partnership in Kitchener was singularly focused in its desire to set up a neighborhood market in a particular neighborhood; private entrepreneurs or vendors may not be as willing or interested in navigating city regulations to set up their business. In other words, the presence of such regulations may have the undesirable, and perhaps unintended, result of interfering in the private market and pushing food entrepreneurs away from setting up healthful food businesses in areas that need them the most. Even slight modifications to the zoning codes and municipal ordinances, such as allowing exceptions to vendors interested in setting up fresh fruit and vegetables vendors in residential neighborhoods, will remove such a barrier.

The second strategy is that of limiting foods that may be unhealthful and less than wholesome for human consumption. Based on the precedents mentioned in Chapter 2 of this PAS Report, we here suggest modifications that planners may wish to consider for their communities. These are not meant to be prescriptive, but simply to illustrate how zoning codes and city ordinances may be modified to encourage creation of a healthy food environment.

Removal of barriers.

- Allow fruit and vegetable markets and stands in all zoning districts of a municipality.

- Allow community gardens as a permissible land use in all zoning districts of a municipality, provided land used for the gardens is found to be nontoxic for cultivation.

- Fast-track the licensing process for fruit and vegetable vendors, including mobile markets and pushcarts, to set up business, such as by providing a waiver of licensing fees if the market is set up in underserved neighborhoods, creating a fast-track licensing process, etc.

Limiting unhealthful foods.

- Limit the density (or number) of fast-food restaurants and other food venues deemed to be unhealthful by the local health commissioner in designated areas.

- Prohibit fast-food restaurants and other food venues deemed to be unhealthful by the local health department to be located within a specific distance of schools and day care centers.

- Prohibit convenience stores and other food stores located within a short distance of schools and day care centers from placing advertisements for cigarettes and unhealthy foods in the windows or exterior facade of stores.

These provisions on limiting or prohibiting unhealthful food destinations could include an exception for fast-food restaurants that obtain a "healthy offerings" certification from the local public health agency. A critical task in such a provision would be establishing with a certain degree of accuracy of what constitutes unwholesome food or what constitutes a "healthy offering." One way to do so would be to work with the local public health commissioner's office to develop an assessment tool to gauge the minimum nutritional quality of healthy foods sold in food destinations, such as restaurant. As part of the licensing process, restaurants would be required to get a "health offerings check" from the commissioner's office to certify that the offerings in the restaurant are healthful. Of course, a number of exceptions could also be allowed. For example, a restaurant would be required to get a check only if locating in certain areas of the city.

CONCLUSION

The profession of planning has always been concerned with the well-being of people and communities. Planners work to ensure people have access to shelter, water, transportation, and jobs. Given the critical role of food for people's well-being and nourishment, it would be negligent of the profession to overlook its role in removing barriers that limit people's access to healthful foods. Although this PAS Report primarily focuses on food en-

The second strategy is that of limiting foods that may be unhealthful and less than wholesome for human consumption.

vironments and healthy eating, we would be remiss if we fail to point out that food is one of many complex influences on individual health. Exercise and physical activity, for example, are significant factors that affect people's health. Without considering the varied factors that influence people's health, planners may not be able to facilitate the health of communities. Finally, food is not the purview of any single discipline. Farmers, nutritionists, planners, business owners— all play a critical role in facilitating people's access to healthful foods. Planners have an especially important role in tying many of these fields by facilitating the planning and design of communities where healthy food systems and healthy eating become possible.

1. In many communities, informal grassroots food policy networks may exist outside of the local government structure of a municipality or state.

2. Support for the survey was provided by the Healthy Eating by Design program of the Robert Wood Johnson Foundation.

3. The survey was advertised through the *Interact*, a biweekly electronic newsletter disseminated to all APA members. Interested APA members were directed to a web link that was available only to APA members.

4. Because of the focus of this report on promoting healthy eating through food planning, we did not include a host of other food-related issues, such as economic development through food businesses.

5. The Community Farm Alliance is a grassroots membership organization whose members include farmers and urban and rural citizens from across Kentucky. The organization works on a broad range of issues that focus on connecting rural farmers to urban residents.

6. The assessment included East Downtown and West Louisville. It was conducted in several phases, spanning 2004-2007. The Community Farm Alliance also conducted a food diary program to document eating behaviors of youth in three Jefferson County middle schools. Brown, Johnson Traditional, and Meyzeek Middle Schools are all located in East Downtown or West Louisville. This project is ongoing, but preliminary analysis revealed some interesting findings. From a random sample of 208 diaries, 93 percent of students averaged one or fewer servings of fruit and one or fewer servings of vegetables per day. Sixty percent of students averaged one or more fast-food meals per day, with some students eating up to three fast-food meals a day (CFA 2007).

7. Separate from the efforts of the Smoketown/Shelby Park Farmers' Market, a federal program also exists to make farmers' markets accessible to WIC recipients. The WIC Farmers Market Nutrition Program was founded by Congress in 1992 and is administered by the state, specifically the Kentucky Department of Agriculture (KDA). Out of Kentucky's 120 counties, KDA administers the grant in 43 counties, not including Jefferson County. The grant is awarded based on successful redemption rates or how many WIC recipients actually use the FMNP money they receive. Unfortunately, a pilot project conducted in 2000 in Jefferson County had relatively few WIC recipients because it was piloted in a middle- to upper-class neighborhood. As a result, the redemption rates were too low to warrant the administration of the program in Jefferson County even though the county has a whole largest concentration of WIC recipients (128,000 families) in the state.

8. In cases where issues of mobility are more severe, a mobile food pantry is operated by Serve Care, a local nonprofit that stops at local parks where people can receive emergency food assistance.

9. Urban Fresh is a business owned and operated by local youth to provide access to healthy, fresh food and to provide economic opportunities. Youth assist the local California Farmers' Market by picking up produce at farms to sell at the city farmers market. Occasionally, the youth even harvest the produce themselves from local farms. The Urban Fresh recruitment process targets former drug-dealing youth to become part of this unique initiative. Based on their skills in sales, knowledge of neighborhood distribution networks, and familiarity with the neighborhood residents, these youth have valuable knowledge to complement local family farmers in finding new markets for fresh food sales. The youth are able to make an honorable living, and citizens gain access to nutritious and affordable local food.

10. Food security is defined as a "limited or uncertain availability of nutritionally adequate and safe foods or limited or uncertain ability to acquire acceptable foods in socially acceptable ways." U.S. Department of Agriculture, which is the source of the data for the Brandeis report, measures food insecurity along a continuum, where food insecurity with hunger indicates a worse condition than food insecurity. See www. ers.usda.gov/Briefing/FoodSecurity/measurement.htm for detailed definitions of food insecurity.

11. A community food plan commissioned by the Massachusetts Avenue Project defines the neighborhood as an area including census tracts 66.01, 67.01 and 69.

12. Start-up costs for the business as well as personnel costs are currently recovered through grant monies and other revenue sources.

List of References and Bibliography

Chapter 1

APA (American Planning Association). 2007. American Planning Association Policy Guide on Community and Regional Food Planning. Prepared for the APA Legislative and Policy Committee. April.

Born, Branden, and Mark Purcell. 2006. "Avoiding the Local Trap: Scale and Food Systems in Planning Research." *Journal of Planning Education and Research* 26, no. 2: 195–207.

Donofrio, Alexander. 2007. "Feeding the City." *Gastronomica: the Journal of Food and Culture* 7, no. 4: 30–41

Kingsolver, Barbara, S. Hopp, and Camille Kingsolver. 2007. *Animal, Vegetable, Miracle: A Year of Food Life*. New York: Harper Collins.

Pollan, Michael. 2006. *The Omnivore's Dilemma: A Natural History of Four Meals*. New York: The Penguin Press.

Pothukuchi, K., and J. Kaufman. 2000. "The Food System: A Stranger to the Planning Field." *Journal of the American Planning Association* 66, no. 2: 113–24.

Schlosser, Eric. 2001. *Fast Food Nation*. New York: Houghton Mifflin Company.

Shiva, Vandana. 2000. *Stolen Harvest: The Hijacking of the Global Food Supply*. London: Zed Books Ltd.

Chapter 2

Arcata, California, City of. 2002. Ordinance no. 1333. An ordinance of the city council of the city of Arcata amending the Arcata municipal code, title IX, the Land use and Development guide, to define restaurants and formula restaurants and to limit the current number of formula restaurants in the commercial and industrial zone districts of the city to nine establishments.

Borron, Sarah Marie. 2003. *Food Policy Councils: Practice and Possibility*. Eugene, Ore.: Congressional Hunger Center.

Brown, Allison. 2001. "Counting Farmers Markets." *Geographical Review* 91, no. 4: 655–75.

Buffalo, New York, City of. Charter and the Code of the City of Buffalo. Updated 12–30–2007. Section 199–4. www.e-codes.generalcode.com.

Caton Campbell, Marcia. 2004. "Building a Common Table: The Role for Planning in Community Food Systems." *Journal of Planning Education and Research* 23, no. 4: 341–55

Concord, Massachusetts, Town of. 2006. Zoning Bylaws. www.concordnet.org/Pages/ConcordMA_BOA/zone/index

———. Zoning Bylaws. Section 4.7.1.Prohibited Uses. www.concordnet.org/Pages/ConcordMA_BOA/zone/sec4.pdf.

Fernandez, Nanny. 2006. "Pros and Cons of a Zoning Diet: Fighting Obesity by Limiting Fast-Food Restaurants." *New York Times*, September 24.

Glosser, D., Jerome Kaufman, and K. Pothukuchi. 2007. "Community and Regional Food Planning." *Planning Advisory Service Memo*. www.planning.org/Pasmemo/previouseditions.htm

Kelvin, Rochelle. 1994. *Community Supported Agriculture: Case Study and Survey*. Kutztown, Pa.: Rodale Institute Research Center.

Kim, Young. 2008. Email communication with Jessica Kozlowski Russell.

Los Angeles, California, City of. 2007. News Release: Fast-Food Interim Control Ordinance Approved by Council Committee: Ordinance Would Give Council Members Perry and Parks Oversight in Planning Process To Help Spur the Development of Diverse Food Choices in South Los Angeles. www.lacity.org/council/cd9/cd9press/cd9cd9press16549545_12122007.pdf

Madison, Wisconsin, City of. 2006. Comprehensive Plan. Adopted by the Common Council on January 17.

Madison, Wisconsin, City of, Metropolitan School District. 2006. Wisconsin Homegrown Lunch. Research, Education, Action and Policy on Food Group (REAP Food Group). www.reapfoodgroup.org/farmtoschool/

Mair, Julie Samia, Matthew Pierce, and Stephen Teret. 2005. "The Use of Zoning to Restrict Fast Food Outlets: A Potential Strategy to Combat Obesity." The Center for Law and the Public's Health at Georgetown and Johns Hopkins Universities. www.publichealthlaw.net/Zoning%20Fast%20Food%20Outlets.pdf

Miedema, Judy Maan. 2008a. Phone interview with Samina Raja. February.

_____. 2008b. *Neighborhoods Markets Initiative: Evaluation Report.* Region of Waterloo Public Health, Health Determinants, Planning and Evaluation Division. February. Waterloo, Canada.

OSU (The Ohio State University). 2000. *The Ohio State University Extension's Urban Gardening Program: 2000* Report. www.brightdsl.net/~cuyahoga/ext00.html

Patel, Ishwarbhai C. 1991. "Gardening's Socioeconomic Impacts: Community Gardening in an Urban Setting." *Journal of Extension* (Winter).

Raja, Samina. 2007. "Growing Green: Empowering Youth, Transforming Neighborhood Food Systems." Prepared for the Massachusetts Avenue Project and the U.S. Department of Agriculture. December 30.

_____. 2000. "Preserving Community Gardens in a Growing Community: A Report on the Community Gardens Planning Process in Madison, Wisconsin." Madison Food System Project Working Paper MFSP–WPS–04. University of Wisconsin–Madison. September.

Raja, Samina, and Angelika Breinlich. 2007. "Designing Healthy Communities, One School at a Time." Prepared for the Healthy Eating by Design–Buffalo project of the Robert Wood Johnson Foundation, Princeton, N.J.

Seattle, Washington, City of. 2005. Toward a Sustainable Seattle (the city's comprehensive plan). www.seattle.gov/DPD/Planning/Seattle_s_Comprehensive_Plan/ComprehensivePlan/default.asp

Vancouver, British Columbia, City of. 2007. Food Charter. http://vancouver.ca/comms-vcs/socialplanning/initiatives/foodpolicy/policy/charter.htm

Waterloo, Ontario, Canada, Regional Council. 2007. A Healthy Community Food System Plan. Public Health for the Waterloo Region. http://chd.region.waterloo.on.ca/web/health.nsf/4f4813c75e78d71385256e5a0057f5e1/54ED787F44ACA44C852571410056AEB0/$file/FoodSystem_Plan.pdf?openelement

Chapter 3

Marin County

Hinds, Alex. 2007. Phone interview with Jessica Kozlowski.

Marin, California, County of. 2007. Countywide Plan. Adopted November 6.

MALT (Marin Agricultural Land Trust). 2007. www.malt.org.

Washburn, Constance. 2008. Phone interview with Samina Raja, July 11.

Madison

Allan, Majid, Branden Born, and Geoff Herbach. eds. 1997. *Fertile Ground: Planning for the Madison/Dane County Food System.* Madison: Department of Urban and Regional Planning, University of Wisconsin–Madison.

Dane, Wisconsin, County of. 2007. Comprehensive Plan. Adopted October.

Dillon, Casey and Martin Harris. 2007. *Counties and Local Food Systems. Ensuring Healthy Foods, Nurturing Health Children.* Washington, D.C.: National Association of Counties Center for Sustainable Communities. www.naco.org/Template.cfm?Section=technical_assistance&template=/ContentManagement/ContentDisplay.cfm&ContentID=24784

Madison, Wisconsin, City of. 2006. Comprehensive Plan. Adopted January 17.

Raja, Samina. 2000. "Preserving Community Gardens in a Growing Community: A Report on the Community Gardens Planning Process in Madison, Wisconsin." September. Madison Food System Project Working Paper MFSP–WPS–04. University of Wisconsin–Madison.

Stevens M., and Samina Raja. 2001. "What's Eating You About What You Eat? Results From a Survey of Madison Area Residents Regarding Their Likes and Concerns About the Local Food System." Madison Food System Working Paper MFSP–WPS–05. University of Wisconsin–Madison.

Stouder, Heather. 2004. "Grocery Stores in City Neighborhoods: Supporting Access To Food Choices, Livable Neighborhoods, And Entrepreneurial Opportunities in Madison, Wisconsin." Office of the Mayor. Madison, Wisconsin. May.

Philadelphia

Adler, David. 2007. Phone interview with Jessica Kozlowski, November 28.

Burton, Hannah, and Duane Perry. 2004. "Stimulating Supermarket Development: A New Day for Philadelphia." Philadelphia, Pa.: The Food Trust. http://thefoodtrust.lightsky.com/pdf/SupermktReport_F.pdf

Chung, Chanjin, and Samuel L. Myers, Jr. 1999. "Do the Poor Pay More for Food? An Analysis of Grocery Store Availability and Food Price Disparities." *The Journal of Consumer Affairs* 33, no. 2: 276–96.

The Food Trust. n.d. Corner Store Campaign. www.thefoodtrust.org/php/programs/corner.store.campaign.php

Perry, Duane. 2001. "The Need for More Supermarkets in Philadelphia." Philadelphia, Pa.: The Food Trust.

_____. 2007. Phone interview with Jessica Kozlowski Russell, November 12.

Raja, Samina, Changxing Ma, and Pavan Yadav. 2008. "Beyond Food Deserts: Measuring and Mapping Racial Disparities in Neighborhood Food Environments." *Journal of Planning Education and Research* 27: 469–82.

Short, Anne, Julie Guthman, and Samuel Raskin. 2007. "Food Deserts, Oases, or Mirages?" *Journal of Planning Education and Research* 26, no. 3: 352–64.

Smith, Patricia. 2007a. Phone interview with Jessica Kozlowski Russell, November 28.

_____. 2007b. E-Mail communication with Jessica Kozlowski Russell, November 28.

TRF (The Reinvestment Fund). 2004. *Fresh Food Financing Initiative: Program Guidelines.* Philadelphia, Pa.: The Reinvestment Fund. www.trfund.com/resource/downloads/applications/FFFI_Program_Guidelines.pdf

_____. 2007. "The Economic Impacts of Supermarkets on their Surrounding Communities: Reinvestment Brief." Philadelphia, Pa.: The Reinvestment Fund and Econsult Corporation. www.trfund.com/resource/downloads/policypubs/supermarkets.pdf

Weinberg, Zy. 2000. "No Place to Shop: The Lack of Supermarkets in Low-Income Neighborhoods." *Race, Poverty, and Environment* (Winter): 22–24

Louisville, Kentucky

Active Living by Design–Louisville (ALBD–Louisville). 2007. www.activelivingbydesign.org.

CFA (Community Farm Alliance). 2007. *Bridging the Divide: Growing Self-Sufficiency in our Food Supply.* Louisville, Ky.: Community Farm Alliance.

Howard, Sarah. 2007. Phone interview by Jessica Kozlowski Russell, September 14.

Raja, Samina, Changxing Ma, and Pavan Yadav. 2008. "Beyond Food Deserts: Measuring and Mapping Food Environments in Erie County." *Journal of Planning Education and Research* 27: 469-82..

Short, Anne, Julie Guthman, and Samuel Raskin. 2007. "Food Deserts, Oases, or Mirages?" *Journal of Planning Education and Research* 27: 469–82.

Portland

Adair, T., A. Burris, L. Kleepsie, D. Moore, M. Moran, V. Rainwater, A. Rossinoff, and E. Young. 2005. *The Spork Report: Increasing the Supply and Consumption of Local Foods in Portland Public Schools*. Portland, Ore.: Portland State University.

Anderson, L., K. Krajnak, L. Libby, M. MacKenzie, S. Malik, and K. Shriver. 2006. *Local Lunches: Planning for Local Produce in Portland Schools*. Portland, Ore.: Portland State University.

Briggs, Suzanne. 2007. Phone interview conducted by Jessica Kozlowski Russell, November 16.

Cohen, Steve. 2007. Phone interviews with Jessica Kozlowski Russell, July and November.

Cordello, Rosemarie. 2007. Phone interview with Jessica Kozlowski Russell, November 27.

DLCD (Portland, Oregon, City of, Department of Land Conservation and Development). 2008. "Measure 49 Guide." January 25.

ODA (Oregon, State of, Department of Agriculture). 2007a. "Historical Perspective: Agriculture's Role in Oregon." Salem, Ore. January.

_____. 2007b. "Present Status of the Industry." Salem, Ore. January.

Pierson, T., and J. Hammer. *Barriers and Opportunities to the Use of Regional and Sustainable Food Products by Local Institutions: A Report to Community Food Matters and the Portland/Multnomah Food Policy Council*. www2.co.multnomah.or.us/County_Management/Sustainability/sustainability_reports/Food%20Policy%20Council%20recomendations%202003.pdf

PMFPC (Portland Multnomah Food Policy Council). 2003. "Food Policy Recommendations." 2003. Office of Sustainable Development, Portland, Oregon.

Portland, Oregon, City of. 2002. Resolution No. 36074. Establish a Portland/Multnomah County Food Policy Council. Adopted by the Council, May 29.

Chapter 4

About Growing Green. Massachusetts Avenue Project. www.mass-ave.org.

About Grassroots Gardens. Grassroots Gardens. www.grassrootsgardens.org.

Buffalo, State University of New York at. 2003. *Food For Growth: A Community Food System Plan for Buffalo's West Side*. Planning Studio Report, Department of Urban and Regional Planning.

Picard, Diane. 2007. Phone interview with Jessica Kozlowski Russell, September 25.

Raja, Samina. 2006. *Growing Green Interim Evaluation Report*. Buffalo, N.Y.: State University of New York.

Raja, Samina, and Angelika Breinlich. 2007. "Designing Healthy Communities, One School at a Time." Prepared for the Healthy Eating by Design–Buffalo project of the Robert Wood Johnson Foundation, Princeton, N.J.

Chapter 5

Algert, Susan, Aditya Agarwal, Douglas Lewis. 2006. "Disparities in Access to Fresh Produce in Low-Income Neighborhoods in Los Angeles." *American Journal of Preventive Medicine* 30, no. 5: 365–70.

Block, Jason, Richard A. Scribner and Karen B. DeSalvo. 2004. "Fast Food, Race/Ethnicity, and Income: A Geographic Analysis." *American Journal of Preventive Medicine* 27, no. 3: 211–17

Buffalo, State University of New York at. 2003. *Food For Growth: A Community Food System Plan for Buffalo's West Side*. Planning Studio Report, Department of Urban and Regional Planning.

Chung, Chanjin, and Samuel L. Myers, Jr. 1999. "Do the Poor Pay More for Food? An Analysis of Grocery Store Availability and Food Price Disparities." *The Journal of Consumer Affairs* 33, no. 2: 276–96.

Lewis, LaVonna Blair, David Sloane, Lori Miller Nascimento, Allison L. Diamant, Joyce Jones Guinyard, Antronette Yancey, Gwendolyn Flynn. 2005. "African–Americans' Access to Healthy Food Options in South Los Angeles Restaurants." *American Journal of Public Health* 95, no. 4: 668–73.

Mari Gallaghar Consulting and Research Group. 2006. *Examining the Impact of Food Deserts on Public Health in Chicago*. Commissioned by the LaSalle Bank, Chicago, Illinois.

Moore, Latetia, and Ana V. Diez Roux. 2006. "Associations of Neighborhood Characteristics with the Location and Type of Food Stores." *American Journal of Public Health* 96, no. 2: 325–31.

Morland, Kimberly, Ana V. Diez Roux, and Steve Wing. 2006. "Supermarkets, Other Food Stores, and Obesity: The Atherosclerosis Risk in Communities Study." *American Journal of Preventive Medicine* 30, no. 4: 333–39.

Morland, Kimberly, Steve Wing, Ana Diez Roux, and Charles Poole. 2002. "Neighborhood Characteristics Associated with Location of Food Stores and Food Service Places." *American Journal of Preventive Medicine* 22, no. 1: 23–29.

Saelens, Brian, Karen Glanz, James Sallis, and Lawrence Frank. 2007. "Nutrition Environment Measures Study in Restaurants (NEMS–R): Development and Evaluation." *American Journal of Preventive Medicine* 32, no. 4: 273–81

Sallis, J. F., R. Nader, and J. Atkins. 1986. "San Diego Surveyed for Heart Healthy Foods and Exercise Facilities." *Public Health Report* 101: 216–18.

Short, Anne, Julie Guthman, and Samuel Raskin. 2007. "Food Deserts, Oases, or Mirages?" *Journal of Planning Education and Research* 26, no. 3: 352–64.

Zenk, Shannon, Amy Shutz, Barbara Israel, Sherman James, Shuming Bao, and Mark Wilson. 2005. "Neighborhood Composition, Neighborhood Poverty, and the Spatial Accessibility of Supermarkets in Detroit." *American Journal of Public Health* 95, no. 4: 660–67.

Chapter 6

APA (The American Planning Association). 2007. American Planning Association Policy Guide on Community and Regional Food Planning. Prepared for the American Planning Association's Legislative and Policy Committee. April.

Pothukuchi, Kami. 2004. "Community Food Assessments: A First Step in Planning for Community Food Security." *Journal of Planning Education and Research* 23: 356–77

Pothukuchi, Kami, Hugh Joseph, Hannah Burton, and Andy Fisher. 2002. *What's Cooking in Your Food System? A Guide to Community Food Assessment*. Venice, Calif.: Community Food Security Coalition.

Key Web Resources

Active Living by Design
www.activelivingbydesign.org/

American Planning Association's Policy Guide on Community and Regional Food Planning
www.planning.org/policyguides/food.htm

Community Food Security Coalition
www.foodsecurity.org

Children's Nutrition and WIC Reauthorization Act of 2004
www.schoolwellnesspolicies.org/resources/Section204LocalWellnessPolicies.pdf

Healthy Eating by Design
www.activelivingbydesign.org/index.php?id=392

United States Department of Agriculture, Center for Nutrition Policy and Promotion
www.cnpp.usda.gov/

Vancouver Food Charter
www.vancouver.ca/commsvcs/socialplanning/initiatives/foodpolicy/tools/pdf/Van_
   Food_Charter_Bgrnd.pdf

World Hunger Year, Food Security Learning Center
www.worldhungeryear.org/fslc/default.asp

Making Great Communities Happen

The American Planning Association provides leadership in the development of vital communities by advocating excellence in community planning, promoting education and citizen empowerment, and providing the tools and support necessary to effect positive change.

506/507. Old Cities/Green Cities: Communities Transform Unmanaged Land. J. Blaine Bonham, Jr., Gerri Spilka, and Darl Rastorfer. March 2002. 123pp.

508. Performance Guarantees for Government Permit Granting Authorities. Wayne Feiden and Raymond Burby. July 2002. 80pp.

509. Street Vending: A Survey of Ideas and Lessons for Planners. Jennifer Ball. August 2002. 44pp.

510/511. Parking Standards. Edited by Michael Davidson and Fay Dolnick. November 2002. 181pp.

512. Smart Growth Audits. Jerry Weitz and Leora Susan Waldner. November 2002. 56pp.

513/514. Regional Approaches to Affordable Housing. Stuart Meck, Rebecca Retzlaff, and James Schwab. February 2003. 271pp.

515. Planning for Street Connectivity: Getting from Here to There. Susan Handy, Robert G. Paterson, and Kent Butler. May 2003. 95pp.

516. Jobs-Housing Balance. Jerry Weitz. November 2003. 41pp.

517. Community Indicators. Rhonda Phillips. December 2003. 46pp.

518/519. Ecological Riverfront Design. Betsy Otto, Kathleen McCormick, and Michael Leccese. March 2004. 177pp.

520. Urban Containment in the United States. Arthur C. Nelson and Casey J. Dawkins. March 2004. 130pp.

521/522. A Planners Dictionary. Edited by Michael Davidson and Fay Dolnick. April 2004. 460pp.

523/524. Crossroads, Hamlet, Village, Town (revised edition). Randall Arendt. April 2004. 142pp.

525. E-Government. Jennifer Evans–Cowley and Maria Manta Conroy. May 2004. 41pp.

526. Codifying New Urbanism. Congress for the New Urbanism. May 2004. 97pp.

527. Street Graphics and the Law. Daniel Mandelker with Andrew Bertucci and William Ewald. August 2004. 133pp.

528. Too Big, Boring, or Ugly: Planning and Design Tools to Combat Monotony, the Too-big House, and Teardowns. Lane Kendig. December 2004. 103pp.

529/530. Planning for Wildfires. James Schwab and Stuart Meck. February 2005. 126pp.

531. Planning for the Unexpected: Land-Use Development and Risk. Laurie Johnson, Laura Dwelley Samant, and Suzanne Frew. February 2005. 59pp.

532. Parking Cash Out. Donald C. Shoup. March 2005. 119pp.

533/534. Landslide Hazards and Planning. James C. Schwab, Paula L. Gori, and Sanjay Jeer, Project Editors. September 2005. 209pp.

535. The Four Supreme Court Land-Use Decisions of 2005: Separating Fact from Fiction. August 2005. 193pp.

536. Placemaking on a Budget: Improving Small Towns, Neighborhoods, and Downtowns Without Spending a Lot of Money. December 2005. 133pp.

537. Meeting the Big Box Challenge: Planning, Design, and Regulatory Strategies. Jennifer Evans–Crowley. March 2006. 69pp.

538. Project Rating/Recognition Programs for Supporting Smart Growth Forms of Development. Douglas R. Porter and Matthew R. Cuddy. May 2006. 51pp.

539/540. Integrating Planning and Public Health: Tools and Strategies To Create Healthy Places. Marya Morris, General Editor. August 2006. 144pp.

541. An Economic Development Toolbox: Strategies and Methods. Terry Moore, Stuart Meck, and James Ebenhoh. October 2006. 80pp.

542. Planning Issues for On-site and Decentralized Wastewater Treatment. Wayne M. Feiden and Eric S. Winkler. November 2006. 61pp.

543/544. Planning Active Communities. Marya Morris, General Editor. December 2006. 116pp.

545. Planned Unit Developments. Daniel R. Mandelker. March 2007. 140pp.

546/547. The Land Use/Transportation Connection. Terry Moore and Paul Thorsnes, with Bruce Appleyard. June 2007. 440pp.

548. Zoning as a Barrier to Multifamily Housing Development. Garrett Knaap, Stuart Meck, Terry Moore, and Robert Parker. July 2007. 80pp.

549/550. Fair and Healthy Land Use: Environmental Justice and Planning. Craig Anthony Arnold. October 2007. 168pp.

551. From Recreation to Re-creation: New Directions in Parks and Open Space System Planning. Megan Lewis, General Editor. January 2008. 132pp.

552. Great Places in America: Great Streets and Neighborhoods, 2007 Designees. April 2008. 84pp.

553. Planners and the Census: Census 2010, ACS, Factfinder, and Understanding Growth. Christopher Williamson. July 2008. 132pp.

554. A Planners Guide to Community and Regional Food Planning: Transforming Food Environments, Facilitating Healthy Eating. Samina Raja, Branden Born, and Jessica Kozlowski Russell. August 2008. 112pp.